THE EASTER SPIRIT

THE EASTER SPIRIT

AN ANTHOLOGY

compiled by
Robert Van de Weyer and Pat Saunders

Darton, Longman and Todd
London
Published in association with
Little Gidding books

First published in 1990 by
Darton, Longman and Todd Ltd
89 Lillie Road, London SW6 1UD

in association with
Little Gidding Books
Little Gidding, Huntingdon PE17 5RJ

Introduction and selection
© 1990 Little Gidding Books

British Library Cataloguing in Publication Data

The Easter spirit: an anthology.
1. English literature. Special subjects: Easter –
Anthologies
I. Van de Weyer, Robert, *1950–* II. Saunders, Pat
820.8'033

ISBN 0–232–51835–1

Designed by Michael R. Carter

Phototypeset by Input Typesetting Ltd, London SW19 8DR

Printed and bound by Courier International Ltd, Tiptree, Essex

Contents

Introduction

Clement of Alexandria, the great father of the Church, declared that through his resurrection 'Christ has turned all our sunsets into dawns'. From the earliest centuries of the Church Easter has been regarded as the most important festival of the Christian year. It is the resurrection of Christ on Easter morning that gives meaning and purpose to his birth, ministry and death.

Yet compared to Christmas, or even Good Friday, it is a strange and even awkward festival – we are never quite sure in which mood to celebrate it. A birth and a death are commonplace events, and the emotions which they engender are relatively familiar. But a man rising from the dead to walk again on earth jolts all our assumptions and ideas about the natural order of things. Should we be fearful, even terrified, as were the disciples when they first discovered the empty tomb? Should we be bewildered, not knowing the nature of the risen Christ and the meaning of his appearance; after all, the gospel accounts themselves seem, to our human eyes, confused, and even contradictory. Or should we be excited, our hearts on fire with joy, as were those who broke bread with the risen Jesus on the road to Emmaus? Perhaps we should experience all these emotions, since the resurrection is both a mystery, far above our human understanding, and also a revelation, illuminating the very essence of life itself.

The prose and poetry in this anthology are responses to this mystery and revelation. We have taken the main events in the Easter story, from Palm Sunday to the meeting on the Emmaus road, and devoted one chapter to each. Many of the pieces are specifically Christian, referring to the events themselves; and as you read them you shall find within each chapter particular spiritual themes recurring. In addition there are passages from the whole range of English literature – novels and diaries, letters and essays – which echo the themes within every sphere of human experience.

The book may be read alone, kept on the bedside table to be dipped into during the early spring. It is also intended for use in group meditation, perhaps during the six weeks of Lent, or through Holy Week: a selection of the pieces in each chapter could be read in turn over the space of an hour or so, interspersed with short periods of silence. Indeed we have ordered the pieces so that the themes are developed through the course of the chapter, to assist meditation. The chapters each begin with a prayer and the relevant Bible reading, and conclude with a hymn (which daring groups may sing) and another prayer.

Compiling the book has been enormously enjoyable and spiritually rewarding: on Easter morning we can now sing 'Christ the Lord is risen today' with even greater conviction and gusto. We pray that you too may find your Easter faith enhanced, and that the Easter spirit may infuse every aspect of your daily life.

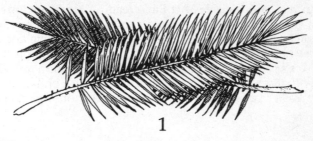

1
Entry into Jerusalem

Take from us, O God, all pride and vanity, all boasting and forwardness; and give us the true courage that shows itself by gentleness, the true wisdom that shows itself by simplicity, and the true power that shows itself by modesty; through Jesus Christ our Lord.

Charles Kingsley (1819–1875)

And when they came nigh to Jerusalem, unto Bethphage and Bethany, at the mount of Olives, he sendeth forth two of his disciples, and saith unto them, Go your way into the village over against you: and as soon as ye be entered into it, ye shall find a colt tied, whereon never man sat; loose him, and bring him. And if any man say unto you, Why do ye this? say ye that the Lord hath need of him; and straightway he will send him hither. And they went their way, and found the colt tied by the door without in a place where two ways met; and they loose him. And certain of them that stood there said unto them, What do ye, loosing the colt? And they said unto them even as Jesus had commanded: and they let them go. And they brought the colt to Jesus, and cast their garments on him; and he sat upon him. And many spread their garments in the way; and others cut down branches off the trees and strewed them in the way. And they that went before, and they that followed, cried, saying,

> Hosanna; Blessed is he that cometh in the name of the Lord:
> Blessed be the kingdom of our father David,
> that cometh in the name of the Lord:
> Hosanna in the highest.

And Jesus entered into Jerusalem, and into the temple: and when he had looked round about upon all things, and now the eventide was come, he went out unto Bethany with the twelve.

Mark 11: 1–11

1 Rejoice Jerusalem

Rejoice Jerusalem, burst into hymns of praise. Praise his Majesty, be grateful to your Benefactor! This yearning to praise is always being discharged by you and always demanded of you. It is promptly discharged and piously demanded. The demand in itself is a joy. Your yearning to grasp blessed truth is its own commendation and the breath of peace settling over the affections brings joys along with the light. 'Light has dawned for the just and joy for the upright of heart. Rejoice in the Lord, you just.' What exchange shall they make for this rejoicing? 'And remember to praise him for holiness.' So delight flows from the light and thanksgiving flows from delight. Delight expanding bursts into praise, and our hearts overflowing cannot but bubble over with the happy intoxication of luminous truth, and inebriated with the flow of sweetness cannot refrain from song.

Gilbert of Hoyland (12th century), *Treatise 3*

2 Palm Sunday

Hark! how the children shrill and high
    Hosanna cry,
Their joys provoke the distant sky,
Where thrones and seraphims reply,
And their own angels shine and sing
    In a bright ring:
    Such young, sweet mirth
    Makes heaven and earth
Join in a joyful symphony.

Henry Vaughan (1622–1695)

—— 3 *Upon the Ass that Bore Our Saviour* ——

Hath only Anger an Omnipotence
                    In Eloquence?
Within the lips of Love and Joy doth dwell
                    No miracle?
Why else had *Baalam's* Ass a tongue to chide
                    His Master's pride?
And thou (Heaven-burthen'd Beast) hast ne'er a word
                    To praise thy Lord?
That he should find a Tongue and vocal Thunder
                    Was a great wonder.
But o methinks 'tis a far greater one
                    That thou find'st none.

Richard Crashaw (c. 1613–1649)

—————— 4 *The Real Pilgrim* ——————

A real pilgrim going to Jerusalem leaves behind his house and land, his wife and children; he divests himself of all that he possesses, so that he can travel light. Similarly, if you wish to be a spiritual pilgrim, you must strip yourself of all your spiritual possessions; your good deeds as well as your bad deeds must be left behind. You must regard yourself as so spiritually poor that you have no confidence in your own actions; instead you must desire only the presence of Jesus, and his profound love. In this way you will be setting your heart wholly on reaching Jerusalem; on obtaining the love of Jesus and such vision of him as he sees fit to give you . . .

You are now on the road, and you know the way. But beware of enemies who will try to obstruct you if they can. Their intention is to uproot from your heart your desire for the love of Jesus, and to turn your heart back to earthly desires. Your chief enemies are bodily desires and foolish fears which can rise up in your heart, and which stifle your desire for the love of God. These are the deadliest enemies. But there are other enemies also who will use every trick to deceive you. There is only one sure way to resist them. Whatever they say, do not believe them, but stride firmly on your way, thinking only of Jesus. And when they persist, say, 'I am nothing, I have nothing, I desire nothing but the love of Jesus' . . .

You are now fast approaching Jerusalem. You have not yet arrived, but you are able to see the city in the distance before you arrive because of the rays of light shining from it. Remember that, although your soul is untroubled by thoughts of this world, you are not yet at the end of the journey, for your soul is not yet clothed in light and set aflame with the fire of love. You are still aware of something beyond your soul's reach, which you neither understand nor possess, but which you ardently desire. This desire is for nothing less than the vision of Jerusalem itself.

Jerusalem symbolizes the perfect love of God, set upon the hill of contemplation. To a soul that has no experience of it, it can seem quite small. But as you continue towards the city, it appears far greater – greater than anything that you could possibly have conceived. And the reward awaiting you in Jerusalem transcends the highest human desire.

Walter Hilton (d. 1395), *The Ladder of Perfection*

―――――――― 5   *Christ's Morality* ――――――――

Now, if we look at the Gospels with the firm intention to discover the *emphasis* of Christ's morality, we shall find that it did not lie at all along the lines laid down by the opinion of highly placed and influential people. Disreputable people who knew they were disreputable were gently told to 'go and sin no more'; the really unparliamentary language was reserved for those thrifty, respectable, and sabbatarian citizens who enjoyed Cæsar's approval and their own. And the one and only thing that ever seems to have roused the 'meek and mild' Son of God to a display of outright physical violence was precisely the assumption that 'business was business.' The money-changers in Jerusalem drove a very thriving trade, and made as shrewd a profit as any other set of brokers who traffic in foreign exchange; but the only use Christ had for these financiers was to throw their property down the front steps of the Temple.

Dorothy L. Sayers (1893–1957), *Unpopular Opinions*

―――――――――― 6 *Our Hero* ――――――――――

Our Lord Jesus Christ, my brethren, is our hero, a hero all the world wants. You know how books of tales are written, that put one man before the reader and shew him off handsome for the most part and brave and call him My Hero or Our Hero. Often mothers make a hero of a son; girls of a sweetheart and good wives of a husband. Soldiers make a hero of a great general, a party of its leader, a nation of any great man that brings it glory, whether king, warrior, statesman, thinker, poet, or whatever it shall be. But Christ, he is the hero. He too is the hero of a book or books, of the divine Gospels. He is a warrior and a conqueror; of whom it is written he went forth conquering and to conquer. He is a king, Jesus of Nazareth king of the Jews, though when he came to his own kingdom his own did not receive him, and now, his people having cast him off, we Gentiles are his inheritance. He is a statesman, that drew up the New Testament in his blood and founded the Roman Catholic Church that cannot fail. He is a thinker, that taught us divine mysteries. He is an orator and poet, as in his eloquent words and parables appears. He is all the world's hero, the desire of nations.

Gerard Manley Hopkins (1844–1889), 'Sermon: on Luke ii. 33'

7 Digging for the Kingdom

Christ came to establish a Kingdom, not to proclaim a set of opinions. Every man entering his Kingdom becomes interested in all its relations, members and circumstances. He cannot separate himself in any wise apart from them. He cannot establish a life or interest apart from theirs . . .

My business, because I am a theologian, and have no vocation except for theology, is not to build, but to dig, to show that economy and politics must have a ground beneath themselves. Our task consists in proclaiming society and humanity to be divine realities, as they stand, not as they may become . . .

We do not suppose that success will necessarily attach to any particular system of human contrivance, but that it will depend on the degree in which we keep close to the true law of human society, which God has ordained. Society is not to be made anew by arrangements of ours, but is to be regenerated by finding the law and ground of its order and harmony, the only secret of its existence, which is God himself. There will be discovered beneath all the politics of the earth, sustaining the order of each country, upholding the charity of each household, a City which has foundations, whose builder and maker is God.

F. D. Maurice (1805–1872), *Politics for the People*

8 The Moral Huntsman

In view of what he plainly said, is it any wonder that all who were rich and prosperous felt a horror of strange things, a swimming of their world at his teaching? Perhaps the priests and the rulers and the rich men understood him better than his followers. He was dragging out all the little private reservations they had made from social service into the light of a universal religious life. He was like some terrible moral huntsman digging mankind out of the snug burrows in which they had lived hitherto. In the white blaze of this kingdom of his there was to be no property, no privilege, no pride and precedence; no motive indeed and no reward but love. Is it any wonder that men were dazzled and blinded and cried out against him? Even his disciples cried out when he would not spare them the light. Is it any wonder that the priests realized that between this man and themselves there was no choice but that he or priestcraft should perish? Is it any wonder that the Roman soldiers, confronted and amazed by something soaring over their comprehension and threatening all their disciplines, should take refuge in wild laughter, and crown him with thorns and robe him in purple and make a mock Cæsar of him? For to take him seriously was to enter upon a strange and alarming life, to abandon habits, to control instincts and impulses, to essay an incredible happiness . . .

Is it any wonder that to this day this Galilean is too much for our small hearts?

H. G. Wells (1866–1946), *The Outline of History*

———— 9 *The Peaceful Kingdom* ————

All that pretend to fight for Christ they are deceived, for his kingdom is not of this world, therefore his servants do not fight. Therefore fighters are not of Christ's kingdom, but are without Christ's kingdom: for his kingdom stands in peace and righteousness; but fighters are in the lust, and all that would destroy men's lives are not of Christ's mind, who came to save men's lives. Christ's kingdom is not of this world; it is peaceable: and all that be in strife are not of his kingdom . . . All such as pretend Christ Jesus, and confess him, and yet run into the use of carnal weapons, wrestling with flesh and blood, throw away the spiritual weapons. They that would be wrestlers with flesh and blood, throw away Christ's doctrine, and flesh is got upon them, and they are weary of their sufferings. Ye that be heirs of the Gospel of Peace which was before the Devil was, live in the Gospel of Peace, seeking the peace of all men, and the good of all men: and live in Christ, who came to save men's lives . . . And all Friends everywhere, this I charge you, which is the word of the Lord God unto you all: Live in peace, in Christ the way of peace, and therein seek the peace of all men, and no man's hurt.

George Fox (1624–1691), *Journal*

It behoves the Christian king in a Christian nation to be, as is right, the people's comfort and a righteous shepherd over the Christian flock. And it behoves him to raise up the Christian faith with all his power and zealously advance and protect God's Church everywhere, and with just law to bring peace and reconciliation to all Christian people, as diligently as he can, and in everything cherish righteousness in the sight of God and the world. For if he cherish justice in the sight of God and the world, through that he himself foremost shall prosper and his subjects similarly. And it behoves him diligently to support those who desire righteousness, and strictly punish those who desire perversity. He must severely correct wicked men with worldly punishment, and he must loathe and suppress robbers and plunderers and despoilers of the world's goods, and sternly resist all God's foes. And with justice he must be both merciful and austere: merciful to the good and stern to the evil. That is the king's right and a kingly custom, and that shall accomplish most in the nation.

Indeed, by what means shall peace and comfort come to God's servants and God's poor, but through Christ and through a Christian king? Through an unwise king, the people will be made wretched not once but very often, because of his misdirection. Through the king's wisdom the people will become prosperous and successful and victorious. And therefore the wise king must extol and exalt the Christian faith and kingship, and he must always repress and condemn heathenism. He must very earnestly attend to book-learning, and carefully keep God's commands and frequently seek out wisdom with the council, if he wish to obey God aright. And if anywhere in the nation anyone be so violent that he will keep no law as he should, but violates the law of God or hinders the law of the people, then it is to be made known to the king, if it is necessary; and then he is immediately to take counsel concerning the compensation and diligently subject him to that which is his duty, even by compulsion if he cannot otherwise. And he is to do what is needful for him if he wish to merit the mercy of God: purify his nation in the sight of God and the world, and frequently meditate what he is to do and what not to do according to God's law. And thus both in life and after life he shall in particular always gain reputation and respect to the extent that he love God's law and abhor injustice, and for his own good willingly attend to divine teaching over and over again. For he who takes little bodily nourishment soon weakens, and he who rarely takes spiritual nourishment will soon severely injure his soul. But he who most often obeys the divine teaching and most diligently keeps it will be blessed.

Wulfstan (d. 1023), *The Institutes of Polity*

11 Courage to Love

We are somewhere very frightened of love without recognizing at all clearly that we are. For absolute love, God's love, makes us fully ourselves, instead of the half people we generally are. And to become fully yourself is a terrible risk. It would commit you to God knows what and lead you God knows where. If I open my heart in simplicity to God's love I might soon find myself in Bangladesh or something of that sort, or I might find myself disagreeing or even agreeing with Mrs Whitehouse. Or letting in God's love might prompt me to join the Campaign for Homosexual Equality, or the Tory Party, or it might lead me actively to support the Tribune Group; it might make me concerned about the oppressed peoples of the Third World or even about my neighbour next door who is lonely. And God's love has been known to make the most respectable people enjoy a pub crawl. And letting in God's love is no guarantee at all that I will necessarily remain an enthusiastic member of the Church of England or even of the Anglo-Catholic set-up. And so, not so much in our minds consciously as in our bones unconsciously, we see to it that when we pray we keep ourselves tied up in knots. It is much safer. Let us keep on the armour of our sophistication and plump for security.

But then of course we miss the glorious liberty of the children of God. We remain half dead, too afraid to know what life is. And missing out on the splendour and warm intimacy of God's love, we become hooked on some compensatory activity like overwork or keeping up with the Jones's, or drink, or sex, or it might even be religiosity and church going. Such compensatory activities don't in practice compensate at all.

H. A. Williams (b. 1919), *Becoming What I Am*

It falls to the lot of those who are engaged in the active and arduous profession of the law to pass their lives in great cities, amidst severe and incessant occupation, requiring all the faculties, and calling forth, from time to time, many of the strongest passions of our nature. In the midst of all this, rivals are to be watched, superiors are to be cultivated, connections cherished; some portion of life must be given to society, and some little to relaxation and amusement. When, then, is the question to be asked, 'What shall I do to inherit eternal life?' what leisure for the altar, what time for God? I appeal to the experience of men engaged in this profession, whether religious feelings and religious practices are not, without any speculative disbelief, perpetually sacrificed to the business of the world? Are not the habits of devotion gradually displaced by other habits of solicitude, hurry, and care, totally incompatible with habits of devotion? Is not the taste for devotion lessened? Is not the time for devotion abridged? Are you not more and more conquered against your warnings and against your will; not, perhaps, without pain and compunction, by the Mammon of life? And what is the cure for this great evil to which your profession exposes you? The cure is, to keep a sacred place in your heart, where Almighty God is enshrined, and where nothing human can enter; to say to the world, 'Thus far shalt thou go, and no further'; to remember you are a lawyer, without forgetting you are a Christian; to wish for no more wealth than ought to be possessed by an inheritor of the kingdom of heaven; to covet no more honour than is suitable to a child of God; boldly and bravely to set yourself limits, and to show to others you have limits, and that no professional eagerness, and no professional activity, shall ever induce you to infringe upon the rules and practices of religion: remember the text; put the great question really, which the tempter of Christ only pretended to put. In the midst of your highest success, in the most perfect gratification of your vanity, in the most ample increase of your wealth, fall down at the feet of Jesus, and say, 'Master, what shall I do to inherit eternal life?'

Sydney Smith (1771–1845), 'The Lawyer that Tempted Christ: A Sermon'

13 The Death of Cardinal Wolsey

Then was he in confession the space of an hour. And when he had ended his confession, Master Kingston bade him good-morrow (for it was about seven of the clock in the morning); and asked him how he did. 'Sir,' quoth he, 'I tarry but the will and pleasure of God, to render unto him my simple soul into his divine hands.' 'Not yet so, sir,' quoth Master Kingston, 'with the grace of God, ye shall live, and do very well; if ye will be of good cheer.' 'Master Kingston, my disease is such that I cannot live; I have had some experience in my disease, and thus it is: I have a flux with a continual fever; the nature whereof is this, that if there be no alteration with me of the same within eight days, then must either ensue excoriation of the entrails, or frenzy, or else present death; and the best thereof is death. And as I suppose, this is the eighth day: and if ye see in me no alteration, then is there no remedy (although I may live a day or twain) but death, which is the best remedy of the three.' 'Nay, sir, in good faith,' quoth Master Kingston, 'you be in such dolour and pensiveness, doubting that thing that indeed ye need not to fear, which maketh you much worse than ye should be.' 'Well, well, Master Kingston,' quoth he, 'I see the matter against me how it is framed; but if I had served God as diligently as I have done the king he would not have given me over in my grey hairs. Howbeit, this is the just reward that I must receive for my worldly diligence and pains that I have had to do him service; only to satisfy his vain pleasure, not regarding my godly duty.'

George Cavendish (1500–1561), *The Life of Cardinal Wolsey*

14 The Counsel of Death

If we seek a reason of the succession and continuance of this boundless ambition in mortal men, we may add to that which hath been already said, that the kings and princes of the world have always laid before them the actions, but not the ends, of those great ones which preceded them. They are always transported with the glory of the one, but they never mind the misery of the other, till they find the experience in themselves. They neglect the advice of God, while they enjoy life, or hope it; but they follow the counsel of Death upon his first approach. It is he that puts into man all the wisdom of the world, without speaking a word, which God, with all the words of his law, promises, or threats, doth not infuse. Death, which hateth and destroyeth man, is believed; God, which hath made him and loves him, is always deferred . . .

It is therefore Death alone that can suddenly make man to know himself. He tells the proud and insolent, that they are but abjects, and humbles them at the instant, makes them cry, complain, and repent, yea, even to hate their forepast happiness. He takes the account of the rich, and proves him a beggar, a naked beggar, which hath interest in nothing but in the gravel that fills his mouth. He holds a glass before the eyes of the most beautiful, and makes them see therein their deformity and rottenness, and they acknowledge it.

O eloquent, just and mighty Death! whom none could advise, thou hast persuaded; what none hath dared, thou hast done; and whom all the world hath flattered, thou only hast cast out of the world and despised.

Walter Raleigh (c. 1552–1618), *History of the World*

────────────── *15   Divine Guidance* ──────────────

That individual and immediate guidance, in which we recognize that 'the finger of God is come unto us', seems to come in, as it were, to complete and perfect the work rough-hewn by morality and conscience. We may liken the laws of our country to the cliffs of our island, over which we rarely feel ourselves in any danger of falling; the moral standard of our social circle to the beaten highway road which we can hardly miss. Our own conscience would then be represented by a fence, by which some parts of the country are enclosed for each one, the road itself at times barred or narrowed. And that divine guidance of which I am speaking could be typified only by the pressure of a hand upon ours, leading us gently to step to the right or the left, to pause or to go forward, in a manner intended for and understood by ourselves alone . . .

The divine guidance is away from self-indulgence, often away from outward success; through humiliation and failure, and many snares and temptations; over rough roads and against opposing forces – always uphill. Its evidence of success is in the inmost, deepest, most spiritual part of our existence.

Caroline Stephen (1834–1909), *Quaker Strongholds*

16 The Poor Jewels

What a monstrous spectre is this man . . . how surprising are his attributes! Poor soul, here for so little, cast among so many hardships, filled with desires so incommensurate and so inconsistent, savagely surrounded, savagely descended, irremediably condemned to prey upon his fellow lives: who should have blamed him had he been of a piece with his destiny and a being merely barbarous? And we look and behold him instead filled with imperfect virtues: infinitely childish, often admirably valiant, often touchingly kind; sitting down, amidst his momentary life, to debate of right and wrong and the attributes of the deity; rising up to do battle for an egg or die for an idea; singling out his friends and his mate with cordial affection; bringing forth in pain, rearing with long-suffering solicitude, his young. To touch the heart of his mystery, we find in him one thought, strange to the point of lunacy: the thought of duty; the thought of something owing to himself, to his neighbour, to his God . . .

It matters not where we look, under what climate we observe him, in what stage of society, in what depth of ignorance, burthened with what erroneous morality; by campfires in Assiniboia, the snow powdering his shoulders, the wind plucking his blanket, as he sits, passing the ceremonial calumet and uttering his grave opinions like a Roman senator; in ships at sea, a man inured to hardship and vile pleasures, his brightest hope a fiddle in a tavern and a bedizened trull who sells herself to rob him, and he for all that simple, innocent, cheerful, kindly like a child, constant to toil, brave to drown, for others; in the slums of cities, moving among indifferent millions to mechanical employments, without hope of change in the future, with scarce a pleasure in the present, and yet true to his virtues, honest up to his lights, kind to his neighbours, tempted perhaps in vain by the bright gin-palace, perhaps long-suffering with the drunken wife that ruins him; in India (a woman this time) kneeling with broken cries and streaming tears, as she drowns her child in the sacred river; in the brothel, the discard of society, living mainly on strong drink, fed with affronts, a fool, a thief, the comrade of thieves, and even here keeping the point of honour and the touch of pity, often repaying the world's scorn with service, often standing firm upon a scruple, and at a certain cost, rejecting riches: – everywhere some virtue cherished or affected, everywhere some decency of thought and carriage, everywhere the ensign of man's ineffectual goodness: – ah! if I could show you this! If I could show you these men and women, all the world over, in every stage of history, under every abuse of error, under every circumstance of failure, without hope, without help, without thanks, still obscurely fighting the lost fight of virtue, still clinging, in the brothel or on the scaffold, to some rag of honour, the poor jewel of their souls!

Robert Louis Stevenson (1850–1894), 'Pulvis et Umbra'

————— 17 *The Progress of Mankind* —————

The progress of mankind on the path of liberty and humanity has been suddenly arrested and its promise discredited by the apostasy of a great people, who, casting off as a disguise their professions of Honour, now openly avow that the ultimate faith of their hearts is in material force . . .

From the consequent miseries, the insensate and interminable slaughter, the hate and filth, we can turn to seek comfort only in the quiet confidence of our souls; and we look instinctively to the seers and poets of mankind, whose sayings are the oracles and prophecies of loveliness and loving kindness. Common diversions divert us no longer; our habits and thoughts are searched by the glare of the conviction that man's life is not the ease that a peace-loving generation has found it or thought to make it, but the awful conflict with evil which philosophers and saints have depicted; and it is in their abundant testimony to the good and beautiful that we find support for our faith, and distraction from a grief that is intolerable constantly to face, nay impossible to face without that trust in God which makes all things possible.

We may see that our national follies and sins have deserved punishment; and if in this revelation of rottenness we cannot ourselves appear wholly sound, we are still free and true at heart, and can take hope in contrition, and in the brave endurance of sufferings that should chasten our intention and conduct.

Robert Bridges (1844–1930), *The Spirit of Man*

18   Strange Meeting

It seemed that out of battle I escaped
Down some profound dull tunnel, long since scooped
Through granites which titanic wars had groined.
Yet also there encumbered sleepers groaned,
Too fast in thought or death to be bestirred.
Then, as I probed them, one sprang up, and stared
With piteous recognition in fixed eyes,
Lifting distressful hands as if to bless.
And by his smile, I knew that sullen hall,
By his dead smile I knew we stood in Hell.
With a thousand pains that vision's face was grained;
Yet no blood reached there from the upper ground,
And no guns thumped, or down the flues made moan.
'Strange friend,' I said, 'here is no cause to mourn.'
'None,' said that other, 'save the undone years,
The hopelessness. Whatever hope is yours,
Was my life also; I went hunting wild
After the wildest beauty in the world,
Which lies not calm in eyes, or braided hair,
But mocks the steady running of the hour,
And if it grieves, grieves richlier than here.
For by my glee might many men have laughed,
And of my weeping something had been left,

Which must die now. I mean the truth untold,
The pity of war, the pity war distilled.
Now men will go content with what we spoiled,
Or, discontent, boil bloody, and be spilled.
They will be swift with swiftness of the tigress.
None will break ranks, though nations trek from progress.
Courage was mine, and I had mystery,
Wisdom was mine, and I had mastery:
To miss the march of this retreating world
Into vain citadels that are not walled.
Then, when much blood had clogged their chariot-wheels,
I would go up and wash them from sweet wells,
Even with truths that lie too deep for taint.
I would have poured my spirit without stint
But not through wounds; not on the cess of war.
Foreheads of men have bled where no wounds were.
I am the enemy you killed, my friend.
I knew you in this dark: for so you frowned
Yesterday through me as you jabbed and killed.
I parried; but my hands were loath and cold.
Let us sleep now . . .'

Wilfred Owen (1893–1918)

───────── 19   *Pilgrimage to Truth* ─────────

A thousand people were crowding together, crying aloud to
Christ and his dear Mother. They prayed that God would guide
them in their search for Truth. None of them was wise enough
to know the way, so they wandered about like animals . . .
Then a ploughman pushed his way through the crowd.

'By St Peter,' he said, 'I know Truth as well as a scholar
knows his books. My own conscience and common sense led
me to the home of Truth, and I am now pledged to serve him
forever, sowing his seed for as long as I am fit to work. I have
been his follower for fifty years, sowing his seed, herding his
animals, harvesting his corn, and looking after his affairs, both
indoors and out. I do whatever Truth asks: dig ditches, sow
and thresh, make clothes and implements, spin and weave.

And he is pleased with my work, paying me well, and sometimes giving me more than I deserve: he is as prompt in paying wages as any poor man could wish. And he is as gentle as a lamb, courteous to all his servants. So if you would like to know where Truth lives, I will show you the way.'

'Thank you, dear Piers,' the pilgrims said, and offered him money to lead them.

'No,' replied Piers, 'I wouldn't dare touch a farthing. Truth would hold it against me if I took money. But if you want to go the right way I will direct you.

'You must first go through Meekness, men and women alike, and continue until you reach Conscience; if you do this, Christ will know that you love God above all things, and that you treat others as you would like them to treat you . . . After that you will go by a farm which you must not enter; it is called Envy, and those inside covet their neighbours' cattle and wives for themselves. You will also see two pairs of stocks, called Theft and Murder; do not stop, but go round them, not looking back when you have passed by. Then you will come to a hill called False Witness, which is thickly wooded with bribes, and is surrounded by money; turn right away from it, and do not gather flowers from its trees, for fear of losing your soul.

'Finally you will arrive at a place called Honesty, where you will see a castle as bright as the sun, with a moat called Mercy, walls of Wisdom, and battlements of Faith. And all the rooms inside are covered, not with lead roofs, but with Love; and their walls are lined with Humility. Each pillar is built with Prayers, and the gates are hung on hinges of Generosity.

'The doorkeeper's name is Grace, and his servant is called Amendment. He will only let you in if you can honestly say these words: "I am sorry for my sins, and I will always remain sorry for them, even if I were made Pope!" ' . . .

'By Christ,' said the thief, 'I know no one in that castle.'

'Nor me, as far as I know,' said the juggler with a monkey.

'God help me,' said the cake-maker; 'if the journey is as difficult as that, I won't go a foot further.'

'But listen,' cried Piers, trying to encourage them; 'Mercy herself is a maiden at the castle, with power over all the others. She and her son are friends of all sinners; so if you put your trust in them, they will help you. But you must go quickly.'

'Ah, I've just purchased a house,' said one, 'and I must go there to look after it.' And he took his leave of Piers.

'I've got five yoke of oxen,' said another, 'so I must go and set them to work. Piers, if you meet Truth, ask him to excuse me.' And he too took his leave.

'I've just got married,' said a third, 'my wife is loose in her ways, and if I were to leave her for several nights she would fall into sin and desert me. So I cannot come.'
'By Jesus,' cried a prostitute, 'I will go with you, Piers. You can say that I am your sister!'
She looked round, and she saw that she and Piers were alone.

William Langland (c. 1332–1400), *Piers the Ploughman*

──── 20 *Jesu Who Ought to be Praised* ────

It were as easy for Jesu
To renew the withered tree
As to wither the new
Were it His will so to do.
  Jesu! Jesu! Jesu!
  Jesu who ought to be praised.

There is no fish in the sea,
There is no flower on the earth,
There is no tree in the wood,
But proclaims His goodness.
  Jesu! Jesu! Jesu!
  Jesu who ought to be praised.

There is no bird on the wing,
There is no animal in the fields,
There is nothing beneath the sun,
But proclaims His goodness.
  Jesu! Jesu! Jesu!
  Jesu who ought to be praised.

Anonymous (Celtic)

Ride on! ride on in majesty!
Hark, all the tribes hosanna cry;
Thy humble beast pursues his road
With palms and scattered garments strowed.

Ride on! ride on in majesty!
In lowly pomp ride on to die;
O Christ, thy triumphs now begin
O'er captive death and conquered sin.

Ride on! ride on in majesty!
The winged squadrons of the sky,
Look down with sad and wondering eyes
To see the approaching sacrifice.

Ride on! ride on in majesty!
In lowly pomp ride on to die;
Bow thy meek head to mortal pain,
Then take, O God, thy power, and reign.

H. H. Milman (1791–1868)

O God, we thank thee for the life and teaching of Jesus; for the new ideals and new hope that he has given to mankind; for his inspiration to the struggling, his comfort to the fallen; for all the strength and vision which he gives to those who try to spread his spirit on earth. Help us to be more truly thankful for all that his life has meant; and grant that we may thus more worthily strive to follow him and make his love known among men; through the same Jesus Christ our Lord.

Westminster School

2

The Upper Room

Lord Jesus Christ, who when thou wast about to institute thy holy Sacrament at the Last Supper didst wash the feet of the apostles, and teach us by thy example the grace of humility: Cleanse us, we beseech thee, from all stain of sin, that we may be worthy partakers of thy holy mysteries; who livest and reignest with the Father and the Holy Ghost, one God, world without end.

The Royal Maundy

Now the first day of the feast of unleavened bread the disciples came to Jesus, saying unto him, Where wilt thou that we prepare for thee to eat the passover? And he said, Go into the city to such a man, and say unto him, The Master saith, My time is at hand; I will keep the passover at thy house with my disciples. And the disciples did as Jesus had appointed them; and they made ready the passover.

Now when the even was come, he sat down with the twelve. And as they did eat, he said, Verily I say unto you, that one of you shall betray me. And they were exceeding sorrowful, and began every one of them to say unto him, Lord, is it I? And he answered and said, He that dippeth his hand with me in the dish, the same shall betray me. The Son of man goeth as it is written of him: but woe unto that man by whom the Son of man is betrayed! it had been good for that man if he had not been born. Then Judas, which betrayed him, answered and said, Master, is it I? He said unto him, Thou hast said.

And as they were eating, Jesus took bread, and blessed it, and brake it, and gave it to the disciples, and said, Take, eat; this is my body. And he took the cup, and gave thanks, and gave it to them, saying, Drink ye all of it; for this is my blood of the new testament, which is shed for many for the remission of sins. But I say unto you, I will not drink henceforth of this fruit of the vine, until that day when I drink it new with you in my Father's kingdom.

And when they had sung a hymn, they went out into the mount of Olives.

Matthew 26: 17–30

Now then go up with him into the large upper room, furnished for supper, and rejoice to share the delights of the meal which brings us salvation. Let love overcome shyness, affection drive out fear, so that he may at least give you an alms from the crumbs of that table when you beg for something. Or stand at a distance and, like a poor man looking to a rich man, stretch out your hand to receive something, let your tears declare your hunger. But when he rises from table, girds himself with the towel and pours water into the basin, consider what majesty it is that is washing and drying the feet of men, what graciousness it is that touches with his sacred hands the feet of the traitor. Look and wait and, last of all, give him your own feet to wash, because the man whom he does not wash will have no part with him.

Why are you in such a hurry to go out now? Wait a little while. Do you see? Who is that, I ask, who is reclining on his breast and bends back his head to lay it in his bosom? Happy is he, whoever he may be. O, I see: his name is John. O John, tell us what sweetness, what grace and tenderness, what light and devotion you are imbibing from that fountain. There indeed are all the treasures of wisdom and knowledge, the fountain of mercy, the abode of loving kindness, the honeycomb of eternal sweetness.

Aelred of Rievaulx (c. 1110–1167), *A Rule of Life for a Recluse*

2 *Christ Our Guest*

Now when we have received our Lord and have him in our body, let us not then let him alone, and get us forth about other things and look no more unto him (for little good could he, that so would serve any guest) but let all our business be about him. Let us by devout prayer talk to him, by devout meditation talk with him. Let us say with the prophet: I will hear what our Lord will speak within me.

For surely if we set aside all other things and attend unto him, he will not fail with good inspirations to speak such things to us within us as shall serve to the great spiritual comfort and profit of our soul. And therefore let us with Martha provide that all our outward business may be pertaining to him, in making cheer to him and to his company for his sake; that is to wit, to poor folk of which he taketh every one, not only for his disciple, but also as for himself. For himself saith: That that you have done to one of the least of these my brethren, you have done it to myself.

And let us with Mary also sit in devout meditation and harken well what our Saviour, being now our guest, will inwardly say unto us. Now have we a special time of prayer, while he that hath made us, he that hath bought us, he whom we have offended, he that shall judge us, he that shall either damn us or save us, is of his great goodness become our guest and is personally present within us, and that for no other purpose but to be sued unto for pardon and so thereby to save us.

Thomas More (1478–1535), *Treatise on the Holy Eucharist*

——————— 3   *Country Communion* ———————

The Country Parson being to administer the sacraments, is at a stand with himself, how or what behaviour to assume for so holy things. Especially at communion times he is in a great confusion, as being not only to receive God, but to break and administer him. Neither finds he any issue in this, but to throw himself down at the throne of grace, saying, Lord, thou knowest what thou didst, when thou appointedst it to be done thus; therefore do thou fulfil what thou didst appoint; for thou art not only the feast, but the way to it.

At the times of the Holy Communion, he first takes order with the churchwardens, that the elements be of the best, not cheap, or coarse, much less ill-tasted, or unwholesome. Secondly, he considers and looks into the ignorance, or carelessness of his flock, and accordingly applies himself with catechizings, and lively exhortations, not on the Sunday of the communion only (for then it is too late) but the Sunday, or Sundays before the communion, or on the eves of all those days.

If there be any, who having not received yet, is to enter into this great work, he takes the more pains with them, that he may lay the foundation of future blessings. The time of every one's first receiving is not so much by years, as by understanding: particularly the rule may be this: when any one can distinguish the sacramental from common bread, knowing the institution, and the difference, he ought to receive, of what age soever. Children and youths are usually deferred too long, under pretence of devotion to the sacrament, but it is for want of instruction; their understandings being ripe enough for ill things, and why not then for better?

For the manner of receiving, as the parson useth all reverence himself, so he administers to none but to the reverent. The feast indeed requires sitting, because it is a feast; but man's unpreparedness asks kneeling. He that comes to the sacrament, hath the confidence of a guest, and he that kneels, confesseth himself an unworthy one, and therefore differs from other feasters: but he that sits, or lies, puts up to an apostle: contentiousness in a feast of charity is more scandal than any posture.

Touching the frequency of the communion, the parson celebrates it, if not duly once a month, yet at least five or six times in the year: as, at Easter, Christmas, Whitsuntide, before and after harvest, and the beginning of Lent.

George Herbert (1593–1633), *The Country Parson*

─────────── 4 *The Holy Communion* ───────────

Not in rich furniture, or fine array,
   Nor in a wedge of gold,
   Thou, who from me wast sold,
  To me dost now thyself convey;
For so thou should'st without me still have been,
   Leaving within me sin:

But by the way of nourishment and strength
    Thou creep'st into my breast;
    Making thy way my rest,
And thy small quantities my length;
Which spread their forces into every part,
    Meeting sin's force and art.

Yet can these not get over to my soul,
    Leaping the wall that parts
    Our souls and fleshly hearts;
But as th' outworks, they may control
My rebel flesh, and carrying thy name,
    Affright both sin and shame.

Only thy grace, which with these elements comes,
    Knoweth the ready way,
    And hath the privy key,
Op'ning the soul's most subtle rooms;
While those to spirits refin'd, at door attend
    Dispatches from their friend.

George Herbert (1593–1633)

5   *One Bread*

This aspect of Christian worship, like every other, finds its culmination in the Eucharist. There, above all, we are to find our unity with Christ, and with one another in Him. All the symbolism of the service insists on this. There we kneel side by side in virtue of our common discipleship. Differences of rank, wealth, learning, intelligence, nationality, race, all disappear; 'we, being many, are one bread.' We receive the food which has, by its consecration, become for us the Body of the Lord, that it may build us up into that Body, so that as different limbs, but one Body, we may be obedient to His will and carry out His purpose.

It is impossible to separate the individual and corporate aspects of the Holy Communion without irreparable damage to both. That such damage is common there is no doubt. There are many extremely devout people who treat this service as in effect the most intimate of private devotions. That at once reduces it to the level of a Mystery Cult. It is the family meal, where the children gather round the table to receive what their Father gives them. And what He gives, through His incarnate Son, is His own nature; in other words, it is love. But if we receive love, of course we become more loving; we are more closely united with our brother-men; for love is the capacity for, and joy in, the union of spirits. 'If a man say that he love God, and hateth his brother, he is a liar.' If a man say that he has received the Body and Blood of the Lord, and is void of love to other men, he is a liar. 'God is Love'; the Body and Blood of Christ are human nature perfected in love by uttermost sacrifice. If we are in fellowship with God we are by that very fact in fellowship with one another. If we are not in fellowship with one another, if we are envious or contemptuous, if we bear hatred or malice, if we are snobbish or exclusive, we are not in fellowship with God.

William Temple (1881–1944), *Personal Religion and the Life of Fellowship*

──────── 6 *The Symbolism of Food* ────────

The symbolism of food plays a large part in all religions, and especially in Christianity. As within the mysteries of the created order we must all take food and give food – more, must take life and give life – we are here already in touch with the 'life-giving and terrible mysteries of Christ', who indwells that order; for all is the sacramental expression of His all-demanding and all-giving Life. We accept our constant dependence on physical food as a natural and inevitable thing. Yet it is not necessarily so: there are creatures which are free from it for long periods of time. But perhaps because of his border-line status, his embryonic capacity for God, man is kept in constant memory of his own fragility, unable to maintain his existence for long without food from beyond himself; his bodily life dependent on the humble plants and animals that surround him, his soul's life on the unfailing nourishment of the life of God. 'I am the Bread of Life that came down from heaven. He that eateth of *this* bread shall live for ever.' Eternal Life is the gift, the self-imparting of the Eternal God. We cannot claim it in our own right.

Evelyn Underhill (1875–1941), *Abba*

7 Sacrament

Before the Altar of the world in flower,
    Upon whose steps thy creatures kneel in line,
We do beseech Thee in this wild Spring hour,
    Grant us, O Lord, thy wine. But not this wine.

Helpless, we, praying by Thy shimmering seas,
    Beside Thy fields, whence all the world is fed,
Thy little children clinging about Thy knees,
    Cry: 'Grant us, Lord, Thy bread!' But not this bread.

This wine of awful sacrifice outpoured;
    This bread of life – of human lives. The Press
Is overflowing, the Wine-Press of the Lord! . . .
    Yet doth he tread the foaming grapes no less.

These stricken lands! The green time of the year
    Has found them wasted by a purple flood,
Sodden and wasted everywhere, everywhere; –
    Not all our tears may cleanse them from that blood.

The earth is all too narrow for our dead,
    So many and each a child of ours – and Thine
This flesh (our flesh) crumbled away like bread,
    This blood (our blood) poured out like wine, like wine.

Margaret Sackville (1881–1963)

This sense that God is so great in goodness, and we so great in glory, as to be His sons, and so rich as to live in communion with Him, and so individually united to Him, that He is in us, and we in Him, will make us do all our duties not only with incomparable joy but courage also. It will fill us with zeal and fidelity, and make us to overflow with praises. For which one cause alone the knowledge of it ought infinitely to be esteemed. For to be ignorant of this, is to sit in darkness, and to be a child of darkness: it maketh us to be without God in the world, exceeding weak, timorous, and feeble, comfortless and barren, dead and unfruitful, lukewarm, indifferent, dumb, unfaithful. To which I may add, that it makes us uncertain. For so glorious is the face of God and true religion, that it is impossible to see it, but in transcendent splendour. Nor can we know that God is till we see Him infinite in goodness. Nothing therefore will make us certain of His Being but His Glory.

To enjoy communion with God is to abide with Him in the fruition of His Divine and Eternal Glory, in all His attributes, in all His thoughts, in all His creatures, in His Eternity, Infinity, Almighty Power, Sovereignty, &c. In all those works which from all Eternity He wrought in Himself; as the generation of His Son, the proceeding of the Holy Ghost, the eternal union and communion of the blessed Trinity, the counsels of His bosom, the attainment of the end of all His endeavours, wherein we shall see ourselves exalted and beloved from all Eternity. We are to enjoy communion with Him in the creation of the world, in the government of Angels, in the redemption of mankind, in the dispensations of His providence, in the incarnation of His Son, in His passion, resurrection and ascension, in His shedding abroad the Holy Ghost, in His government of the Church, in His judgment of the world, in the punishment of His enemies, in the rewarding of His friends, in Eternal Glory. All these therefore particularly ought to be near us, and to be esteemed by us as our riches; being those delectable things that adorn the house of God which is Eternity; and those living fountains, from whence we suck forth the streams of joy, that everlastingly overflow to refresh our souls.

Thomas Traherne (1637–1674), *Centuries*

9 The Chalice

I heard a radiant ring, with no tongue,
intercede for men, though it spoke
without argument or strident words.
The peaceful treasure pleaded for mankind:
'Heal me, save me, helper of souls.'
May men understand the mysterious saying
of the red gold and, as the ring said,
wisely entrust their salvation to God.

Anonymous (Anglo-Saxon), 'Riddles'

10 A Hymn

Drop, drop, slow tears
    and bathe those beauteous feet,
Which brought from heaven
    the news and Prince of peace:
Cease not, wet eyes,
    his mercies to entreat;
To cry for vengeance
    sin doth never cease:
In your deep floods
    drown all my faults and fears;
Nor let his eye
    see sin, but through my tears.

Phineas Fletcher (1582–1650)

11   Our Courteous Lord

Because of the supreme friendship of our courteous Lord, he tenderly protects us while we are in sin: in secret he touches us and reveals our sins to us by the gentle light of mercy and grace. But we, seeing ourselves so foul, think God may be angry with us because of our sins. Then the Holy Spirit stirs us to contrition and prayer, and our whole desire is to amend ourselves and appease God's anger, so that we may find both rest of soul and ease of conscience. We hope that God has forgiven us our sins; and it is true that he has. It is then that our courteous Lord shows himself to our soul, welcoming it with joy and good cheer as though it were a friend who has been in pain and in prison, saying: 'My beloved, I am glad that you have come to me in your trouble. I have always been with you; and now you see how I love you and we are made one in bliss.' Thus our sins are forgiven by grace and mercy, and our soul is joyfully and honourably received, just as it will be when it enters heaven.

Julian of Norwich (c. 1342–1420), *Revelations of Divine Love*

12   The Sum of All Friendships

So that to your question, how far a dear and perfect friendship is authorized by the principles of Christianity? The answer is ready and easy. It is warranted to extend to all mankind; and the more we love, the better we are and the greater our friendships are, and the nearer we are to God; let them be as dear and let them be as perfect, and let them be as many as you can; there is no danger in it; only where the restraint begins, there begins our imperfection; it is not ill that you entertain brave friendships and worthy societies; it were well if you could *love* and if you could *benefit* all mankind; for I conceive that is the sum of all friendships.

Jeremy Taylor (1613–1667), *Friendship*

13   *The Dove of Peace*

Why should we hate and destroy one another? Are we not all
the creatures of one God, redeemed by one Lord Jesus Christ?
This should provoke us to love and peace one towards another.
If God have revealed more light of the Gospel to one than to
another, shall the more knowing trample the ignorant under his
feet? We should carry ourselves loving and meek one towards
another, with patience persuading and exhorting the contrary
minded, proving if at any time, God will turn their hearts, by
this means the great incendiary of the world, an enforced,
enraged conscience, would be at rest. What is more near and
dear than our consciences? If that be enraged, who can appease
it? If that be satisfied, what content, joy or peace like unto it,
or what more mild, more gentle or loving? Therefore, how
tender ought we to be in cases of conscience? It is a lion if
enraged, a lamb if appeased; it is all honey, or all gall; enraged,
it is like the wild boar of the forest; pleased, it is like the dove
from the ark, no greater friend, no greater foe.

Richard Overton (17th century), *The Arraignment of Mr
Persecution*

14   *Inviting a Friend to Supper*

Tonight, grave sir, both my poor house and I
Do equally desire your company;
Not that we think us worthy such a guest,
But that your worth will dignify our feast
With those that come; whose grace make that seem
Something, which else could hope for no esteem.
It is the fair acceptance, sir, creates
The entertainment perfect, not the cates.
Yet shall you have, to rectify your palate,
An olive, capers, or some better salad
Ushering the mutton; with a short-legged hen,
If we can get her, full of eggs, and then

Lemons, and wine for sauce; to these a coney
Is not to be despaired of, for our money;
And though fowl be scarce, yet there are clerks,
The sky not falling, think we may have larks,
I'll tell you of more, and lie, so you will come! . . .

Ben Jonson (1572–1637)

──────── 15   *The Fruit of Friendship* ────────

A principal fruit of friendship is the ease and discharge of the
fullness and swellings of the heart, which passions of all kinds
do cause and induce. We know diseases of stoppings and suffo-
cations are the most dangerous in the body, and it is not much
otherwise in the mind . . . No receipt openeth the heart but a
true friend, to whom you may impart griefs, joys, fears, hopes,
suspicions, counsels, and whatsoever lieth upon the heart to
oppress it in a kind of civil shrift or confession.
   It is a strange thing to observe how high a rate great kings
and monarchs do set upon this fruit of friendship whereof we
speak – so great, as they purchase it many times at the hazard
of their own safety and greatness. For princes, in regard of the
distance of their fortune from that of their subjects and servants,
cannot gather this fruit, except (to make themselves capable
thereof) they raise some persons to be as it were companions
and almost equals to themselves, which many times sorteth to
inconvenience. The modern languages give unto such persons
the name of *favourites*, as if it were matter of grace, or conversation. But the Roman name attaineth the true use and cause
thereof, naming them *partners in care*, for it is that which tieth
the knot. And we see plainly that this hath been done, not by
weak and passionate princes only, but by the wisest and most
politic that ever reigned; who have oftentimes joined to themselves some of their servants, whom both themselves have
called *friends*, and allowed others likewise to call them in the
same manner, using the word which is received between private
men . . .

Men have their time, and die many times in desire of some things which they principally take to heart: the bestowing of a child, the finishing of a work, or the like. If a man have a true friend, he may rest almost secure that the care of those things will continue after him. So that a man hath as it were two lives in his desires. A man hath a body, and that body is confined to a place; but where friendship is, all offices of life are as it were granted to him and his deputy, for he may exercise them by his friend.

Francis Bacon (1561–1626), 'Of Friendship'

—————— 16   *Direct Communication* ——————

Sometimes I fancy an immense separation, and sometimes, as at present, a direct communication of spirit with you. That will be one of the grandeurs of immortality – there will be no space and consequently the only commerce between spirits will be by their intelligence of each other – when they will completely understand each other – while we in the world merely comprehend each other in different degrees – the higher the degree of good, so higher is our Love and friendship . . . The reason why I do not feel at the present moment so far from you is that I remember your ways and manners and actions; I know your manner of thinking, your manner of feeling; I know what shape your joy or your sorrow would take; I know the manner of your walking, standing, sauntering, sitting down, laughing, punning and every action so truly that you seem near to me. You will remember me in the same manner – and the more when I tell you that I shall read a passage of Shakespeare every Sunday at ten o'clock – you read one at the same time and we shall be as near each other as blind bodies can be in the same room.

John Keats (1795–1821), Letter to his brother

17 *Faithful in Friendship*

I wonder sometimes if I have been unfaithful in my friendships; so many have come and gone, not through any active breach or loss of kind feeling, but from the fact that we have each become different people; and as we became different our points of intimate contact have diminished. It was Emerson, I think, who maintained that for sincerity in friendship, change must be recognized – and accepted; and the real test of the genuineness of a friendship, when circumstances have brought about separation, is whether one does or does not regret that the friendship was ever formed. In very few of my friendships has that sense of regret followed; over all the rest, when the period of intimacy has ended, I have retained a lively feeling of gratitude for benefits received, and to some, whom I never now meet or even hear from, my thoughts go constantly, still registering the old affection of the days when meeting was an exciting pleasure and parting always a regret.

Laurence Housman (1865–1959), *The Unexpected Years*

18 *Fame and Friendship*

FAME is a food that dead men eat, –
I have no stomach for such meat.
In little light and narrow room,
They eat it in the silent tomb,
With no kind voice of comrade near
To bid the feaster be of cheer.

But Friendship is a nobler thing, –
Of Friendship it is good to sing.
For truly, when a man shall end,
He lives in memory of his friend,
Who doth his better part recall
And of his fault make funeral.

Austin Dobson (1840–1921)

Poor human race that must
Feed on pain, or choose another dish
And hunger worse.

There is also a cup of pain, for
You to drink all up, or,
Setting it aside for sweeter drink,
Thirst evermore.

I am thy friend. I wish
You to sup full of the dish
I give you and the drink,
And so to fatness come more than you think
In health of opened heart, and know peace.

Grief spake these words to me in a dream. I thought
He spoke no more than grace allowed
And no less than truth.

Stevie Smith (1902–1971)

20 *A Hermit's Song*

I long, O generous Son of God,
    Ancient and eternal King,
For a hidden hut in wilds untrod,
    Where thy praises I may sing.

A swift, sweet lark of plumage grey
    Chanting songs of love beside me.
A stream to wash my sins away
    Where thy Spirit has sanctified me.

A few true comrades I next would seek
   To mingle their words with mine in prayer.
Men of wisdom, kind and meek,
   Together we thy love declare.

Trout we'll catch and hens we'll keep,
   And bees to give us honey sweet.
Wool we'll weave from three white sheep,
   And ox-hide we'll clasp around our feet.

A church of wood and thatch we'll build,
   A home for Christ in bread and wine.
Let it with songs of praise be filled,
   And love in every corner shine.

Anonymous (Celtic)

———— Hymn: Alleluia! Sing to Jesus! ————

Alleluia! sing to Jesus!
   His the sceptre, his the throne;
Alleluia! his the triumph,
   His the victory alone:
Hark! the songs of peaceful Sion
   Thunder like a mighty flood;
Jesus out of every nation
   Hath redeemed us by his blood.

Alleluia! not as orphans
   Are we left in sorrow now;
Alleluia! he is near us,
   Faith believes, nor questions how:
Though the cloud from sight received him,
   When the forty days were o'er,
Shall our hearts forget his promise,
   'I am with you evermore'?

Alleluia! bread of angels,
  Thou on earth our food, our stay;
Alleluia! here the sinful
  Flee to thee from day to day:

Intercessor, friend of sinners,
  Earth's redeemer, plead for me,
Where the songs of all the sinless
  Sweep across the crystal sea.

Alleluia! king eternal,
  Thee the Lord of Lords we own;
Alleluia! born of Mary,
  Earth thy footstool, heaven thy throne:
Thou within the veil hast entered,
  Robed in flesh, our great High Priest;
Thou on earth both priest and victim
  In the eucharistic feast.

William Chatterton Dix (1837–1898)

O thou who hast prepared a place for my soul, prepare my soul for that place. Prepare it with holiness; prepare it with desire; and even while it sojourneth upon earth, let it dwell in heaven with thee, beholding the beauty of thy countenance and the glory of thy saints, now and for evermore.

Joseph Hall (1574–1656)

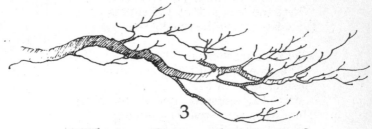

3
The Garden of Gethsemane

O Lord our God, grant us, we beseech thee, patience in troubles, humility in comforts, constancy in temptations, and victory over all our spiritual foes. Grant us sorrow for our sins, thankfulness for thy benefits, fear of thy judgement, love of thy mercies, and mindfulness of thy presence; now and for evermore.

John Cosin (1594–1672)

And he came out, and went, as he was wont, to the mount of Olives; and his disciples also followed him. And when he was at the place, he said unto them, Pray that ye enter not into temptation. And he was withdrawn from them about a stone's cast, and kneeled down, and prayed, saying, Father, if thou be willing, remove this cup from me: nevertheless, not my will, but thine, be done. And there appeared an angel unto him from heaven, strengthening him. And being in an agony he prayed more earnestly: and his sweat was as it were great drops of blood falling down to the ground. And when he rose up from prayer, and was come to his disciples, he found them sleeping for sorrow, and said unto them, Why sleep ye? rise and pray, lest ye enter into temptation.

And while he yet spake, behold a multitude, and he that was called Judas, one of the twelve, went before them, and drew near unto Jesus to kiss him. But Jesus said unto him, Judas, betrayest thou the Son of man with a kiss? When they which were about him saw what would follow, they said unto him, Lord, shall we smite with the sword? And one of them smote the servant of the high priest, and cut off his right ear. And Jesus answered and said, Suffer ye thus far. And he touched his ear, and healed him. Then Jesus said unto the chief priests, and captains of the temple, and the elders, which were come to him, Be ye come out, as against a thief, with swords and staves? When I was daily with you in the temple, ye stretched forth no hands against me: but this is your hour, and the power of darkness.

Then took they him, and led him, and brought him into the high priest's house. And Peter followed afar off.

Luke 22:39–54

Eight ancient olive trees still mark the site of Gethsemane; not improbably they witnessed that memorable and mysterious scene referred to in Hebrews 5.7–8. And what a scene was that! It had stood alone in unique and unapproachable wonder, had it not been followed by 15 hours of even greater mystery.

The strongest words in Greek language are used to tell of the keen anguish through which the Saviour passed within those garden walls. 'He *began* to be sorrowful'; as if in all His past experiences He had never known what sorrow was! 'He was sore amazed'; as if His mind were almost dazed and overwhelmed. 'He was very heavy', His spirit stooped beneath the weight of His sorrows, as afterwards His body stooped beneath the weight of His cross; or the word may mean that He was so distracted with sorrow as to be almost beside Himself. And the Lord Himself could not have found a stronger word than He used when He said, 'My soul is exceeding sorrowful, even unto death.'

But the evangelist Luke gives us the most convincing proof of His anguish when he tells us that His sweat, like great beads of blood, fell upon the ground, touched by the slight frost, and in the cold night air. The finishing touch is given in the words which tell of His 'strong crying and tears' . . .

There are comparatively few to whom Jesus does not say, at some time in their lives, 'Come and watch with me'. He takes us with Him into the darksome shadows of the winepress, though there are recesses of shade, at a stone's cast, where He must go alone. Let us not misuse the precious hours in the heavy slumbers of insensibility. There are lessons to be learnt there which can be acquired nowhere else; but if we heed not His summons to watch with Him, it may be that He will close the precious opportunity by bidding us sleep on and take our rest, because the allotted term has passed, and the hour of a new epoch has struck. If we fail to use for prayer and preparation the sacred hour that comes laden with opportunities for either; if we sleep instead of watching with our Lord: what hope have we of being able to play a noble part when the flashing lights and the trampling feet announce the traitor's advent? Squander the moments of preparation, and you have to rue their loss through all the coming years!

F. B. Meyer (1847–1929), *The Way into the Holiest*

Then said King Edmund, very brave as he was: 'This I desire and wish with my heart, that I alone should not be left, after my beloved thegns, who with wives and children were suddenly slain in their beds by these pirates. It was never my custom to take flight, but I would rather die for my own country if I must; and Almighty God knows that I would never turn away from his worship, nor from his true love, whether I die or live.'

After these words he turned to the messenger that Ivar had sent to him and said to him, unafraid: 'You would certainly deserve death now, but I would not dirty my clean hands in your filthy blood, for I follow Christ, who set us an example thus; and I will cheerfully be slain by you if God so ordains it. Go very quickly now and say to your savage lord: "Edmund will never while living submit to the heathen war-leader, Ivar, unless he first submit in this land to Christ the Saviour in faith." '

Then the messenger went away quickly and met the savage Ivar on the way hastening to Edmund with his entire army, and told the wicked man how he was answered. Then Ivar resolutely commanded the men of the war-ships that they should all seize only the king, who had scorned his behest, and immediately bind him. Well, then when Ivar came, King Edmund stood within his hall, mindful of the Saviour, and threw aside his weapons; he would imitate the example of Christ, who forbade Peter to fight against the savage Jews with weapons. So, then those wicked men bound Edmund and insulted him shamefully, and beat him with cudgels, and afterwards led the faithful king thus to a tree rooted in the ground, and tied him to it with tight bonds, and afterwards flogged him with whips for a long time; and amidst the floggings he unceasingly called on Christ the Saviour with true faith; and then, because of his faith, the heathen became insanely angry because he called on Christ to help him. Then, as if for sport, they shot at him with darts, until he was entirely covered with their missiles, like the bristles of a hedgehog, just as Sebastian was. When the wicked pirate Ivar saw that the noble king would not renounce Christ, but ever called on him with steadfast faith, he ordered him to be beheaded; and the heathens did so. While he still called on Christ the heathens dragged the saint away to slaughter and with one blow struck off his head, and his blessed soul went to Christ. There was at hand a certain man, hidden from the heathens by God, who heard all this and afterwards told it just as we tell it here.

Aelfric (c. 955–1010), *Lives of the Saints*

————— 3 For Whom the Bell Tolls —————

Perchance he for whom this bell tolls, may be so ill, as that he knows not it tolls for him. And perchance I may think myself so much better than I am, as that they who are about me, and see my state, may have caused it to toll for me, and I know not that. The Church is catholic, universal, so are all her actions. All that she does, belongs to all. When she baptises a child, that action concerns me; for that child is thereby connected to that head which is my head too, and engrafted into that body whereof I am a member. And when she buries a man, that action concerns me. All mankind is of one author, and is one volume. When one man dies, one chapter is not torn out of the book, but translated into a better language; and every chapter must be so translated. God employs several translators: some pieces are translated by age, some by sickness, some by war, some by justice; but God's hand is in every translation, and his hand shall bind up all our scattered leaves again for that library where every book shall lie open to one another. As therefore the bell that rings to a sermon, calls not upon the preacher only, but upon the congregation to come; so this bell calls us all: but how much more me, who am brought so near the door by this sickness . . . No man is an island, entire of itself. Every man is a piece of the continent, a part of the main. If a clod be washed away by the sea, Europe is the less, as well as if a promontory were, as well as if a manner of thy friends, or of thine own were. Any man's death diminishes me, because I am involved with mankind. And therefore never send to know for whom the bell tolls; it tolls for thee.

John Donne (1572–1631), *Devotions upon Emergent Occasions*

4 Forgive Me, O Lord

Forgive me O Lord; O Lord, forgive my sins, the sins of my youth, and my present sins, the sin that my parents thrust upon me, original sin, and the sins that I cast upon my children, in an ill example; actual sins, sins which are manifest to all the world, and sins which I have so laboured to hide from the world, and that now they are hid from mine own conscience, and mine own memory. Forgive me my crying sins, and my whispering sins, the sins of uncharitable hate, and sins of unchaste love . . .

Forgive me my sins, all my sins, and I will put Christ to no more cost, nor thee to more trouble, for any reprobation or malediction that lay upon me, otherwise than as a sinner. I ask but an application, not an extension of that benediction, 'Blessed are they whose sins are forgiven'. Let me be but so blessed, that I shall envy no man's blessedness. Say thou to my sad soul, 'Son, be of good comfort, thy sins are forgiven thee.' Let me be so blessed, that I shall envy no man's blessedness. Say thou to my sad soul, 'Son, be of good comfort, thy sins are forgiven thee.'

John Donne (1572–1631), 'Sermon preached to the King, at Whitehall, the first Sunday in Lent'

5 The Pain of Fear

I can with difficulty endure the days but I frankly dread the nights. The second part of almost every night of my life is shot through with such mental pain, fear and horror that I frequently have to wake myself up in order to restore some sort of balance. If I don't manage to do that it quite often takes me three or four hours after waking to recover anything like a normal attitude towards life.

My physical health is reasonably good. I have enough of this world's goods for all my needs and am not conscious of any particular unconfessed sins. I have a very wonderful wife who stands by me steadfastly but I cannot help knowing that my almost continuous pain must be a burden to her. It is only during the last few weeks that I have been seriously assaulted by the thought that it isn't worth trying any more, I am too tired to make further effort and I really do not see the slightest ray of hope at the end of this very long tunnel. I think what chiefly worries me, apart from the sense of the loss of God, is the gradual failure of my own powers to love and be concerned about other people. It is true that perfect love casts out fear, but it is revoltingly true that constant fear and tension cast out love. All pain, especially of the mental kind, seems to me to make one more self-centred.

J. B. Phillips (1906–1982), *The Wounded Healer*

---

6 *De Profundis*

Out of my soul's depth to thee my cries have sounded:
Let thine ears my plaints receive, on just fear grounded.
Lord, should'st thou weigh our faults, who's not confounded?

But with grace thou censur'st thine when they have erred,
Therefore shall thy blessed name be loved and feared.
E'en to thy throne my thoughts and eyes are reared.

Thee alone my hopes attend, on thee relying;
In thy sacred word I'll trust, to thee fast flying,
Long ere the watch shall break, the morn descrying.

In the mercies of our God who live secured,
May of full redemption rest in him assured,
Their sin-sick souls by him shall be recured.

Thomas Campion (1567–1620)

It is indeed possible that you may find such an edge and eagerness upon your spirit as may lead you to imagine that all opposition will immediately fall before you. But alas! I fear that in a little time these enemies which seemed to be slain at your feet, will revive, and recover their weapons, and renew the assault in one form or another. And perhaps your most painful combats may be with such as you had thought most easy to be vanquished, and your greatest danger may arise from some of those enemies from whom you had apprehended the least; particularly from pride, and from indolence of spirit; from a secret alienation of heart from God, and from an indisposition for conversing with Him, through an immoderate attachment to things seen and temporal, which may be oftentimes exceeding dangerous to your salvation, though perhaps they be not absolutely and universally prohibited. In a thousand of these instances you must learn to deny yourself, or you cannot be Christ's disciple . . .

Amidst all the oppositions of earth and hell, look upward, and look forward, and you will feel your heart animated by the view. Your general is near: He is near to aid you: He is near to reward you. When you feel temptations press the hardest, think of Him who endured even the cross itself for your rescue. View the fortitude of your divine leader, and endeavour to march on in His steps. Hearken to His voice, for He proclaims it aloud, 'Behold I come quickly, and my reward is with me. Be thou faithful unto death, and I will give thee a crown of life.' And oh, how bright will it shine, and how long will its lustre last! When the gems that adorn the crowns of monarchs, and pass (instructive thought) from one royal head to another, through succeeding centuries, are melted down in the last flame, it is a crown of glory which fadeth not away.

Philip Doddridge (1702–1751), *The Rise and Progress of Religion in the Soul*

Afflictions quicken us to prayer. It is a pity it should be so; experience testifies that a long course of ease and prosperity, without painful changes, has an unhappy tendency to make us cold and formal in our secret worship; but troubles rouse our spirits, and constrain us to call upon the Lord in good earnest, when we feel the need to that help which we only can have from him.

They are useful, and in a degree necessary, to keep alive in us a conviction of the vanity and unsatisfying nature of the present world, and all its enjoyments; to remind us that this is not our rest, and to call our thoughts upwards, where our true treasure is, and where our conversation ought to be. When things go on much to our wish, our hearts are too prone to say, It is good to be here . . .

Afflictions evidence to ourselves, and manifest to others, the reality of grace. And when we suffer as Christians, exercise some measure of that patience and submission, and receive some measure of these supports and supplies, which the Gospel requires and promises to believers, we are more confirmed that we have not taken up with mere notions; and others may be convinced that we do not follow cunningly devised fables. They likewise strengthen by exercise our graces: as our limbs and natural powers would be feeble if not called to daily exertion; so the graces of the Spirit would languish, without something provided to draw them out to use. And, to say no more, they are honourable, as they advance our conformity to Jesus our Lord, who was a man of sorrows for our sake.

John Newton (1725–1807), *Cardiphonia*

9   *Seasons of Loneliness*

In all seasons of loneliness remember the Lord will stand by you and help you. Loneliness has its trials, but it has great blessings belonging to it. We need loneliness for the purpose of training. How God trained in loneliness the great men of old, down to him that is the greatest of all that have been born of women! How many Christian saints have been trained in intense loneliness, voluntary or involuntary, as the case might be! The Lord 'took him aside from the multitude' to give him the natural gifts of hearing and speech; so He takes us apart if He wishes us to learn His will . . .

We only want a place where we can kneel down and pray, and then the gospel message is sure to go forward. We may not see its progress, but it will work, as a voice on the mountain-top detaches the avalanches from summits and precipices beyond. It is a good thing for us not to have our own liking in the place of settlement. God puts us just where it is best for us to be by taking us out of our own will and judgement. It is for us to exult as we feel ourselves to be swimming in the wide ocean of His love.

R. M. Benson (1824–1915), Letters to Father O'Neill

10   The Hand of Mystery

There are hours, and they come to us all at some period of life or other, when the hand of Mystery seems to lie heavy on the soul – when some life-shock scatters existence, leaves it a blank and dreary waste henceforth for ever, and there appears nothing of hope in all the expanse which stretches out, except that merciful gate of death which opens at the end – hours when the sense of misplaced or ill-requited affection, the feeling of personal worthlessness, the uncertainty and meanness of all human aims, and a doubt of all human goodness, unfix the soul from all its old moorings – and leave it drifting – drifting over the vast Infinitude, with an awful sense of solitariness. Then the man whose faith rested on outward Authority and not on inward life, will find it give way: the authority of the Priest: the authority of the Church: or merely the authority of a document proved by miracles and backed by prophecy: the soul – conscious life hereafter – God – will be an awful desolate Perhaps. Well! in such moments you doubt all – whether Christianity be true: whether Christ was man, or God, or a beautiful fable. You ask bitterly, like Pontius Pilate, What is Truth? In such an hour what remains? I reply Obedience. Leave those thoughts for the present. Act – be merciful and gentle – honest: force yourself to abound in little services: try to do good to others: be true to the Duty that you know. *That* must be right whatever else is uncertain. And by all the laws of the human heart, by the word of God, you shall not be left to doubt. Do that much of the will of God which is plain to you, and 'You shall know of the doctrine, whether it be of God.'

F. W. Robertson (1816–1853), 'Sermon preached March 2, 1851'

– 11   Written in Northampton County Asylum –

I am! yet what I am, who cares or knows?
My friends forsake me, like a memory lost.
I am the self-consumer of my woes;
They rise and vanish, an oblivious host,
Shadows of life, whose very soul is lost.
And yet I am, – I live, – though I am tossed

Into the nothingness of scorn and noise,
Into the living sea of waking dream,
Where there is neither sense of life, nor joys,
But the huge shipwreck of my own esteem
And all that's dear. Even those I loved the best
Are strange, nay, they are stranger than the rest.

I long for scenes where never man has trod,
For scenes where woman never smiled nor wept,
There to abide with my creator, God,
And sleep as I in childhood sweetly slept,
Full of high thoughts, unborn. So let me die –
The grass below; above, the vaulted sky.

John Clare (1793–1864)

Can I see another's woe,
And not be in sorrow too?
Can I see another's grief,
And not seek for kind relief?

Can I see a falling tear,
And not feel my sorrow's share?
Can a father see his child
Weep, nor be with sorrow fill'd?

Can a mother sit and hear
An infant groan an infant fear?
No, no! never can it be!
Never, never can it be!

And can he who smiles on all
Hear the wren with sorrows small,
Hear the small bird's grief & care,
Hear the woes that infants bear,

And not sit beside the nest,
Pouring pity in their breast;
And not sit the cradle near,
Weeping tear on infant's tear;

And not sit both night & day,
Wiping all our tears away?
O, no! never can it be!
Never, never can it be!

He doth give his joy to all;
He becomes an infant small;
He becomes a man of woe;
He doth feel the sorrow too.

Think not thou canst sigh a sigh
And thy maker is not by;
Think not thou canst weep a tear
And thy maker is not near.

O! he gives to us his joy
That our grief he may destroy;
Till our grief is fled & gone
He doth sit by us and moan.

William Blake (1757–1827), *Songs of Innocence*

───────── *13 Reason and Nature* ─────────

To learn the way of dying well we must learn the way to die
without fear. And yet how I should prove that death is not to
be feared, I cannot well tell, seeing the whole power of nature
showeth that of all things death is most fearful: and to reason
against nature, it were peradventure not so hard as vain. For
what can reason prevail, if nature resist? It is a thing too far
above man's power to strive or to wrestle with nature, her
strength passeth the might of our will, what help soever we
take of reason or of authority: neither counsel nor command-
ment hath place, where nature doth her uttermost.

Thomas Lupset (1495–1530), *The Way of Dying Well*

───────── *14 Everything Has Its Shadow* ─────────

And then suffering, bodily suffering such as I've known for
three years. It has changed forever everything – even the *appearance* of the world is not the same – there is something added.
Everything has its shadow. Is it right to resist such suffering? Do
you know I feel it has been an immense privilege? Yes, in spite
of all. How blind we little creatures are! It's only the fairy
tales we *really* live by. If we set out upon a journey, the more
wonderful the treasure, the greater the temptations and perils
to be overcome. And if someone rebels and says, Life isn't
good enough on those terms, one can only say: 'It *is*!' Don't
misunderstand me. I don't mean a 'thorn in the flesh' – it's a
million times more mysterious. It has taken me three years to

understand this – to come to see this. We resist, we are terribly frightened. The little boat enters the dark fearful gulf and our only cry is to escape – 'put me on land again.' But it's useless. Nobody listens. The shadowy figure rows on. One ought to sit still and uncover one's eyes.

Katherine Mansfield (1888–1923), Letter to J. Middleton Murry

--------- 15   *The Great Renunciation* ---------

To every man comes, sooner or later, the great renunciation. For the young, there is nothing unattainable; a good thing desired with the whole force of a passionate will, and yet impossible, is to them not credible. Yet, by death, by illness, by poverty, or by the voice of duty, we must learn, each one of us, that the world was not made for us, and that, however beautiful may be the things we crave, Fate may nevertheless forbid them. It is the part of courage, when misfortune comes, to bear without repining the ruin of our hopes, to turn away our thoughts from vain regrets. This degree of submission to Power is not only just and right: it is the very gate of wisdom.

But passive renunciation is not the whole of wisdom; for not by renunciation alone can we build a temple for the worship of our own ideals. Haunting foreshadowings of the temple appear in the realm of imagination, in music, in architecture, in the untroubled kingdom of reason, and in the golden sunset magic of lyrics, where beauty shines and glows, remote from the touch of sorrow, remote from the fear of change, remote from the failures and disenchantments of the world of fact. In the contemplation of these things the vision of heaven will shape itself in our hearts, giving at once a touchstone to judge the world about us, and an inspiration by which to fashion to our needs whatever is not incapable of serving as a stone in the sacred temple.

Except for those rare spirits that are born without sin, there is a cavern of darkness to be traversed before that temple can be entered. The gate of the cavern is despair, and its floor is paved with the gravestones of abandoned hopes. There Self must die; there the eagerness, the greed of untamed desire must be slain, for only so can the soul be freed from the empire of Fate. But out of the cavern the Gate of Renunciation leads again to the daylight of wisdom, by whose radiance a new insight, a new joy, a new tenderness, shine forth to gladden the pilgrim's heart.

Bertrand Russell (1872–1970), 'A Free Man's Worship'

16 A Fine Teacher

I can picture one teacher there – I can't recall her name. She was short and spare, and I remember her eager jutting chin. Quite unexpectedly one day (in the middle, I think, of an arithmetic lesson) she suddenly launched forth on a speech on life and religion. 'All of you,' she said, 'every *one* of you – will pass through a time when you will face despair. If you never face despair, you will never have faced, or become, a Christian, or known a Christian life. To be a Christian you must face and accept the life that Christ faced and lived; you must enjoy things as he enjoyed things; be as happy as he was at the marriage at Cana, know the peace and happiness that it means to be in harmony with God and with God's will. But you must also know, as he did, what it means to be alone in the Garden of Gethsemane, to feel that all your friends have forsaken you, that those you love and trust have turned away from you, and that *God himself* has forsaken you. Hold on then to the belief that that is *not* the end. If you love, you will suffer, and if you do not love, you do not know the meaning of a Christian life.'

She then returned to the problems of compound interest with her usual vigour, but it is odd that those few words, more than any sermon I have ever heard, remained with me, and years later they were to come back to me and give me hope at a time when despair had me in its grip. She was a dynamic figure, and also, I think, a *fine* teacher; I wish I could have been taught by her longer.

Agatha Christie (1890–1976), *An Autobiography*

17   *That Vacation*

That vacation! Shall I ever forget it? I think not . . . My heart almost died within me; miserable longings strained its chords. How long were the September days! How silent, how lifeless! How vast and void seemed the desolate premises! How gloomy the forsaken garden! . . .

Indeed there was no way to keep well under the circumstances. At last a day and night of peculiarly agonising depression were succeeded by physical illness, I took perforce to my bed. About this time the Indian summer closed and the equinoctial storms began; and for nine dark and wet days, of which the hours rushed on all turbulent, deaf, dishevelled – bewildered with sounding hurricane – I lay in a strange fever of the nerves and blood. Sleep went quite away. I used to rise in the night, look round for her, beseech her earnestly to return. A rattle of the window, a cry of the blast only replied – Sleep never came!

I err. She came once, but in anger. Impatient of my importunity she brought with her an avenging dream. By the clock of St. Jean Baptiste, that dream remained scarce fifteen minutes – a brief space, but sufficing to wring my whole frame with unknown anguish; to confer a nameless experience that had the hue, the mien, the terror, the very tone of a visitation from eternity. Between twelve and one that night a cup was forced to my lips, black, strong, strange, drawn from no well, but filled up seething from a bottomless and boundless sea. Suffering, brewed in temporal or calculable measure, and mixed for mortal lips, tastes not as this suffering tasted. Having drank and woke, I thought all was over: the end come and passed by. Trembling fearfully – as consciousness returned – ready to cry out on some fellow-creature to help me, only that I knew no fellow-creature was near enough to catch the wild summons – Goton in her far distant attic could not hear – I rose on my knees in bed. Some fearful hours went over me: indescribably was I torn, racked and oppressed in mind. Amidst the horrors of that dream, I think the worst lay here. Methought the well-loved dead, who had loved *me* well in life, met me elsewhere, alienated: galled was my inmost spirit with an unutterable sense of despair about the future. Motive there was none why I should try to recover or wish to live; and yet quite unendurable was the pitiless and haughty voice in which Death challenged me to engage his unknown terrors. When I tried to pray I could only utter these words – 'From my youth up Thy terrors have I suffered with a troubled mind.'

Charlotte Brontë (1816–1855), *Villette*

18   *I Fled Him*

I fled Him, down the nights and down the days;
I fled Him, down the arches of the years;
I fled Him, down the labyrinthine ways
   Of my own mind; and in the mist of tears
I hid from Him, and under running laughter,
      Up vistaed hopes I sped;
      And shot, precipitated,
Adown Titanic glooms of chasmed fears,
   From those strong Feet that followed, followed after.
     But with unhurrying chase,
     And unperturbèd pace,
   Deliberate speed, majestic instancy,
    They beat – and a Voice beat
    More instant than the Feet –
'All things betray thee, who betrayest Me.' . . .

   Halts by me that footfall:
   Is my gloom, after all,
Shade of His hand, outstretched caressingly?
   'Ah, fondest, blindest, weakest,
   I am He Whom thou seekest!
Thou dravest love from thee, who dravest Me.'

Francis Thompson (1859–1907), 'The Hound of Heaven'

Alone in my little hut in the forest
I have prepared for death.
Without moving I have been on a long journey
Towards my heavenly home.

I have trodden down my evil passions,
Stamped upon anger and greed.
I have cast aside jealousy and fear,
Leaving them by the wayside.

At times my pace has been bold and fast
Along the gospel way.
At times I have crawled on bended knee
Crying for forgiveness.

Now my journey is almost finished,
My creator comes to fetch me.
Alone I came to my hut in the forest,
And alone in death I shall leave it.

Anonymous (Celtic)

20 If I Stoop

If I stoop
Into a dark tremendous sea of cloud,
It is but for a time; I press God's lamp
Close to my breast; its splendour, soon or late,
Will pierce the gloom: I shall emerge one day.

Robert Browning (1812–1889), 'Paracelsus V'

Rock of ages, cleft for me,
Let me hide myself in thee;
Let the water and the blood,
From thy riven side which flowed,
Be of sin the double cure:
Cleanse me from its guilt and power.

Not the labours of my hands
Can fulfil thy law's demands;
Could my zeal no respite know,
Could my tears for ever flow,
All for sin could not atone:
Thou must save, and thou alone.

Nothing in my hand I bring,
Simply to thy cross I cling;
Naked, come to thee for dress;
Helpless, look to thee for grace;
Foul, I to the fountain fly;
Wash me, Saviour, or I die.

While I draw this fleeting breath,
When my eyelids close in death,
When I soar through tracts unknown,
See thee on thy judgement throne;
Rock of ages, cleft for me,
Let me hide myself in thee.

A. M. Toplady (1740–1778)

O merciful God, be Thou unto me a strong tower of defence, I humbly entreat Thee. Give me grace to await Thy leisure, and patiently to bear what Thou doest unto me; nothing doubting or mistrusting Thy goodness towards me, for Thou knowest what is good for me better than I do. Therefore do with me in all things what Thou wilt; only arm me, I beseech Thee, with Thine armour, that I may stand fast; above all things, taking to me the shield of faith; praying always that I may refer myself wholly to Thy will, abiding Thy pleasure and comforting myself in those troubles which it shall please Thee to send me, seeing such troubles are profitable for me; and I am assuredly persuaded that all Thou doest cannot but be well; and unto Thee be all honour and glory.

Lady Jane Grey (1537–1554)

4

Golgotha

O Lord Jesu Christ, take us to thyself, draw us with cords to the foot of thy cross: for we have no strength to come, and we know not the way. Thou art mighty to save, and none can separate us from thy love. Bring us home to thyself, for we are gone astray. We have wandered; do thou seek us. Under the shadow of thy cross let us live all the rest of our lives, and there we shall be safe.

Frederick Temple (1821–1902)

And they bring him unto the place Golgotha, which is, being interpreted, The place of a skull. And they gave him to drink wine mingled with myrrh: but he received it not. And when they had crucified him, they parted his garments, casting lots upon them, what every man should take. And it was the third hour, and they crucified him. And the superscription of his accusation was written over, THE KING OF THE JEWS. And with him they crucify two thieves; the one on his right hand, and the other on his left. And the Scripture was fulfilled, which saith, And he was numbered with the transgressors.

And they that passed by railed on him, wagging their heads, and saying, Ah, thou that destroyest the temple, and buildest it in three days, save thyself, and come down from the cross. Likewise also the chief priests mocking said among themselves with the scribes, He saved others; himself he cannot save. Let Christ the King of Israel descend now from the cross, that we may see and believe. And they that were crucified with him reviled him.

And when the sixth hour was come, there was darkness over the whole land until the ninth hour. And at the ninth hour Jesus cried with a loud voice, saying, Eloi, Eloi, lama sabachthani? which is, being interpreted, My God, my God, why hast thou forsaken me? And some of them that stood by, when they heard it, said, Behold, he calleth Elijah. And one ran and filled a sponge full of vinegar, and put it on a reed, and gave him to drink, saying, Let alone; let us see whether Elijah will come to take him down. And Jesus cried with a loud voice, and gave up the ghost. And the veil of the temple was rent in twain from the top to the bottom.

And when the centurion, which stood over against him, saw that he so cried out, and gave up the ghost, he said, Truly this man was the Son of God.

Mark 15:22–39

1 The Strength of Christ

Where is the strength of Christ? . . . Surely his strength is in his hands, for his hands were nailed to the arms of the cross. But what strength is there in such weakness, and what height in so great a humiliation? What is there to be venerated in this abjection? In truth the mystery of his strength is hidden by weakness; it is concealed by humility, and made secret by abjection.

O hidden strength! A man hanging on a cross lifts the weight of eternal death; a man fixed on wood frees the world from everlasting death. O hidden power! A man condemned with thieves rescues mankind condemned with devils; a man stretched out on a tree of shame draws all things to himself. O mysterious strength! One soul breathing forth in suffering, draws innumerable souls from hell; one man submitting to the death of the body, destroys the death of souls.

Anselm (c. 1033–1109), *Meditation on the Redemption of Mankind*

2 The Dream of the Rood

Many years ago – the memory abides –
I was felled to the ground at the forest's edge,
Severed from my roots. Enemies seized me,
Made of me a mark of scorn for criminals to mount on;
Shoulder-high they carried me and set me on a hill.
Many foes made me fast there. Far off then I saw
The King of all mankind coming in great haste,
With courage keen, eager to climb me.
I did not dare, against my Lord's dictate,
To bow down or break, though I beheld tremble
The earth's four corners. I could easily
Have felled his foes; yet fixed and firm I stood.

Then the young Hero – it was God Almighty –
Strong and steadfast, stripped himself for battle;
He climbed up on the high gallows, constant in his purpose,
Mounted it in sight of many, mankind to ransom.
Horror seized me when the Hero clasped me,
But I dared not bow or bend down to earth,
Nor falter, nor fall; firm I needs must stand.
I was raised up a Rood, a royal King I bore,
The High King of Heaven: hold firm I must.
They drove dark nails through me, the dire wounds still show,
Cruel gaping gashes, yet I dared not give as good.
They taunted the two of us; I was wet with teeming blood,
Streaming from the warrior's side when he sent forth his spirit.
High upon that hill helpless I suffered
Long hours of torment; I saw the Lord of Hosts
Outstretched in agony; all embracing darkness
Covered with thick clouds the corpse of the World's Ruler;
The bright day was darkened by a deep shadow,
All its colours clouded; the whole creation wept,
Keened for its King's fall; Christ was on the Rood.
Yet warriors from afar eagerly came speeding
To where he hung alone. All this I beheld.

Anonymous (Anglo-Saxon)

───────── 3 *Woefully Arrayed* ─────────

Woefully arrayed,
My blood, man,
For thee ran,
It may not be nayed:
My body blue and wan,
Woefully arrayed.

Behold me, I pray thee, with all thine whole reason,
And be not hard-hearted for this encheason,
That I for thy soul's sake was slain in good season,
Beguiled and betrayed by Judas' false treason,
    Unkindly entreated,
    With sharp cords sore fretted,
    The Jews me threated,
  They mowed, they spitted and despised me
  Condemned to death, as thou mayst see.

Thus naked am I nailed, O man, for thy sake.
I love thee, then love me. Why sleepest thou? Awake!
Remember my tender heart-root for thee brake,
With pains my veins constrained to crack.
    Thus was I defaced,
    Thus was my flesh raced,
    And I to death chased,
  Like a lamb led unto sacrifice,
  Slain I was in most cruel wise.

Of sharp thorn I have worn a crown on my head,
So rubbed, so bobbed, so rueful, so red;
Sore pained, sore strained, and for thy love dead,
Unfeigned, not deemed, my blood for thee shed;
    My feet and hands sore
    With sturdy nails bore.
    What might I suffer more
  Than I have suffered, man, for thee.
  Come when thou wilt and welcome to me!

Dear brother, none other thing I desire
But give me thy heart free, to reward mine hire.
I am he that made the earth, water and fire.
Satan, that sloven, and right loathly sire,
    Him have I overcast
    In hell-prison bound fast,
    Where aye his woe shall last.
  I have purveyed a place full clear
  For mankind, whom I have bought dear.

Anonymous (Medieval)

4 Kicking at Destiny

Not only those who suffer cruelly, like Christ, but all of us,
however soft our circumstances to an outward eye, kick at the
destiny to which we are tied, and wriggle on the nails of our
easy crucifixion. 'If only I were somewhere else – if I were
untied from this difficult marriage – if I were released from this
routine – if I could be freed from anxiety – if my health did not
cramp my spirits – if only . . . then,' we say, not merely, which
is obvious, 'I should be more comfortable,' but, 'then I could
begin to do something, instead of merely existing'; then, we
may even dare to say, 'then I could do something for God.'
This is the great deception of the devil, to stop us loving,
praying, working, now. It may be God's will you should fight
your way out of your misfortunes; it cannot be his will that you
should make them a reason to put off living as a child of God.

Austin Farrer (1904–1968), *Lord I Believe*

5 The World a Crucifix

On June 7th, 1917, I was running to our lines half mad with
fright, though running in the right direction, thank God,
through what had been once a wooded copse. It was being
heavily shelled. As I ran I stumbled and fell over something. I
stopped to see what it was. It was an undersized, underfed
German boy, with a wound in his stomach and a hole in his
head. I remember muttering, 'You poor little devil, what had
you got to do with it? not much great blonde Prussian about
you.' Then there came light. It may have been pure imagination,
but that does not mean that it was not also reality, for what is
called imagination is often the road to reality. It seemed to me
that the boy disappeared and in his place there lay the Christ
upon his cross, and cried, 'Inasmuch as ye have done it unto
the least of these my little ones ye have done it unto me.' From
that moment on I never saw a battlefield as anything but a
crucifix. From that moment on I have never seen the world as
anything but a crucifix.

G. A. Studdert-Kennedy (1883–1929), *The Word and the Work*

6 Crucifying Myself

The Lord crucifies my wisdom and my will every way. But I must be crucified as the thieves. All my bones must be broken, for there is still in me that impatience with wisdom which would stir when the tempter says, 'Come down from the cross.' It is not for us to know the times and seasons, the manner and mystical means of God's working, but only to hunger and thirst and lie passive before the great Potter. In short, I begin to be content to be a vessel of clay or of wood, so I may be emptied of self and filled with my God, my all. Don't give up your confident hope: it saves still secretly, and has a present and, by and by will have a great recompence of reward.

John Fletcher (1729–1785), Letter to Henry Brooke

7 Good Friday

Am I a stone, and not a sheep,
   That I can stand, O Christ, beneath Thy cross,
   To number drop by drop Thy blood's slow loss,
And yet not weep?

Not so those women loved
   Who with exceeding grief lamented Thee;
   Not so fallen Peter weeping bitterly;
Not so the thief was moved;

Not so the Sun and Moon
   Which hid their faces in a starless sky,
   A horror of great darkness at broad noon –
I, only I.

Yet give not o'er,
  But seek Thy sheep, true Shepherd of the flock;
  Greater than Moses, turn and look once more
And smite a rock.

Christina Rossetti (1830–1894)

———————— 8   *Withered Leaves* ————————

Comfort is it by which, in the midst of all our sorrows, we are strengthened and made the better able to bear them all out. And who is there, even the poorest creature among us, but in some degree findeth some comfort, or some regard, at somebody's hands? For if that be not left, the state of that party is said to be like the tree, whose leaves and whose fruit are all beaten off quite, and itself left bare and naked both of the one and of the other.

And such was our Saviour's case in these his sorrows this day; and that so, as what is left the meanest of the sons of men, was not left him: not a leaf. Not a leaf! Leaves I may well call all human comforts and regards, whereof he was then left clean desolate. His own, they among whom he had gone about all his life long, healing them, teaching them, feeding them, doing them all the good he could, it is they that cry, 'Not him, no, but Barabbas rather. Away with him, his blood be upon us and our children.' It is they that in the midst of his sorrows shake their head at him and cry, 'Ah thou wretch'; they that in his most disconsolate estate and cry 'Eli, Eli', in most barbarous manner deride him, and say, 'Stay, and you shall see Elias come presently and take him down.' And this was their regard.

But these were but withered leaves. They that on earth were nearest to him of all, the greenest leaves and likest to hang on and to give him some shade, even of them some bought and sold him, others denied and forswore him, but all fell away and forsook him. Not a leaf left.

But leaves are but leaves, and so are all earthly stays. The fruit then, the true fruit of the vine indeed, the true comfort in all heaviness, is from above, is divine consolation. But even that was in this his sorrow this day, bereft him too. And that was his most sorrowful complaint of all others: not that his friends upon earth, but that his Father from heaven had forsaken him, that neither heaven nor earth yielded him any regard; but that between the passioned powers of his soul, and whatsoever might any ways refresh him, there was a traverse drawn, and he left in the estate of a weather-beaten tree, all desolate and forlorn. Evident, too evident, by that his most dreadful cry, which at once moved all the powers in heaven and earth, 'My God, my God, why hast thou forsaken me?' Weigh well that cry, consider it well, and tell me if ever there were cry like to that of his. Never the like cry, and therefore never the like sorrow.

Lancelot Andrewes (1555–1626), 'Sermon 2 Of the Passion: Good Friday 1604'

9 Murderers of Christ

Look at every vice, pain, and disorder in human nature; it is in itself nothing else but the spirit of the creature turned from the universality of love to some self-seeking or own will in created things. So that love alone is, and only can be, the cure of every evil, and he that lives in the purity of love is risen out of the power of evil into the freedom of the one spirit of heaven. The schools have given us very accurate definitions of every vice, whether it be covetousness, pride, wrath, envy, etc., and shown us how to conceive them as notionally distinguished from one another. But the Christian has a much shorter way of knowing their nature and power and what they all are and do in and to himself. For call them by what names you will, or distinguish them with ever so much exactness, they are all, separately and jointly, just that same one thing, and all do that same one work as the scribes, the pharisees, hypocrites, and rabble of the Jews who crucified Christ were all but one and the same thing and all did one and the same work, however different they were in outward names. If you would therefore have a true sense of the nature and power of pride, wrath, covetousness, envy, etc., they are in their whole nature nothing else but the murderers and crucifiers of the true Christ of God; not as the High Priests did many hundred years ago, nailing His outward humanity to an outward cross, but crucifying afresh the Son of God, the holy Immanuel, who is the Christ that every man crucifies as often as he gives way to wrath, pride, envy, or covetousness, etc. For every temper or passion that is contrary to the new birth of Christ and keeps the holy Immanuel from coming to life in the soul is, in the strictest truth of the words, a murderer and killer of the Lord of life. And where pride and envy and hatred, etc., are suffered to live, there the same thing is done as when Christ was killed and Barabbas was saved alive.

William Law (1686–1761), *The Spirit of Love*

10 The Last Habitation

The grave is full of horror, the house of the dead is the habitation of sadness, for the body receiveth no comfort, when it cometh to lodge in this last and farthest inn. When our feet step upon that shore, we are robbed of all our honours, stripped out of all our gay attires, spoiled of all our gold and silver, forsaken by our friends, fled from by our kinsfolks, yea, abhorred to be looked upon by our own children: nothing is left us but a poor mantle of linen to hide our nakedness; that is the last apparel we must wear, and when that is worn out, we must be turned out of all.

A dreadful thing therefore would it be to dwell in this land of everlasting silence and darkness, but that Christ himself hath gone thither before us. How infinitely are we bound to him, that (in this battle of death) we are not thrust upon any danger, but what he hath gone through. How above measure doth he love us, to try the ice first, before he suffer us to venture over? He went into the grave before us, to show that we all must follow him . . .

Suffer us, O Lord, not to repine, whether in the morning, at noon, or at midnight, that is to say, in our cradle, in our youth, or old age, we go to take our long sleep; but let us make this reckoning of our years, that if we can live no longer, that is unto us our old age; for he that liveth so long as thou appointest him (though he die in the pride of his beauty) dieth an old man. Since then that worms must be our last companions, and that the pillows upon which we are to rest forever, are within but dead men's skulls, whereof should we be proud? Why should we disdain the poorest beggar, when the hand that sways a sceptre, and the hand that holds a sheep-hook, being found together in the earth are both alike? What madness is it so to pamper the flesh with curious meats, and costly wines, when, do what we can, we do but fatten it for crawling vermin? What folly is it, to clothe our body in sumptuous attires, when (let them be never so gorgeous) we shall carry with us but a winding-sheet? Why do we bathe our limbs in sweet waters, and embalm our bodies with rich perfumes, when no carrion in the world can smell more noisome than must our carcases? Blessed therefore be the sepulchre that held our Saviour's body, since it is a book wherein we may learn how to contemn this foolish love of ourselves. Happy was thy burial (O Jesus) that prepared our way to our last habitation.

Thomas Dekker (c. 1572–1632), *Four Fowls of the Noah's Ark*

—————— 11 Hell and Heaven ——————

What is hell, what is damnation, but an exclusion from thy presence? 'Tis the loss of that which gives the regions of darkness all their horror . . . O when wilt thou scatter this melancholy darkness? When shall the shadows flee before thee? When shall the cheerful glory of thy grace dawn upon my mind at thy approach? I shall revive at thy light; my vital spirits will confess thy presence. Grief and anxiety will vanish before thee, and immortal joys surround my soul.

Where thou art present, heaven and happiness ensue; hell and damnation fills the breast where thou art absent. While God withdraws I am encompassed with darkness and despair; the sun and stars shine with an uncomfortable lustre; the faces of my friends grow tiresome; the smile of angels would fail to cheer my languishing spirit. I grow unacquainted with tranquility; peace and joy are empty sounds to me, and words without a meaning.

Tell me not of glory and pleasure – there are no such things without God. When He withdraws, what delight can these trifles afford? All that amuses mankind are but dreams of happiness, shadows and fantasies. What compensation can they make for an infinite good departed? All nature cannot repair my loss; heaven and earth would offer their treasures in vain. Not all the kingdoms of this world, nor the thrones of archangels, could give me a recompence for an absent God.

O where can my grief find redress? Whence can I draw satisfaction, when the fountain of joy seals up its streams? My sorrows are hopeless till He return. Without Him my night will never see a dawn, but extend to everlasting darkness. Contentment and joy will be eternal strangers to my breast. Had I all things within the compass of creation to delight me, his frowns would blast the whole enjoyment. Unreconciled to God, my soul would be forever at variance with itself.

Even now, while I believe thy glory hidden from me with only a passing eclipse, and while I wait for thy return as for the dawning day, my soul suffers inexpressible agonies at the delay. The minutes seem to linger and the days are lengthened into ages. But Lord, what keener anguish should I feel if I thought thy presence had totally forsaken me, if I imagined thy glory should no more arise on my soul! My spirits fail at the thought: I cannot face the dreadful apprehensions of my God forever gone. Is it not hell in its most horrid prospect, eternal darkness and the undying worm, infinite ruin and irreparable damage? Compared to this, what were all the plagues that earth could threaten or hell invent? What are disgrace, and poverty, and pain? What are all that mortals fear, real or imaginary evils? They are nothing compared to the terrors raised by the thought of losing my God.

O thou who art my boundless treasure, my infinite delight, my all, my ineffable portion, can I part with thee? I may see without light and breathe without air sooner than be blessed without my God. Happiness separate from thee is a contradiction, an impossibility (if I dare speak it) to Omnipotence itself. I feel a flame which the most glorious creation could not satisfy, an emptiness which nothing but infinite love could fill. I must find thee or weary myself in an eternal pursuit. Nothing shall divert me in the endless search, no obstacle shall frighten me back, no allurement withhold me; nothing shall flatter or relieve my impatience. My bliss, my heaven, my all depends on my success in this. Show me where thou art, O my God; conduct me into thy presence, and let my love confine me there forever.

Elizabeth Rowe (1674–1737), *Devout Exercises of the Heart*

12   The Artful Devil

How inconsistent is the devil! How artfully does he strive to
keep poor souls from Christ! Sometimes he labours to drive
poor souls into despair; sometimes to presumption. These are
the two rocks against which he would fain have poor souls to
make shipwreck of faith and a good conscience. I pray God to
enable you to steer a middle course.

May you see your misery, and at the same time see your
remedy in the cross and wounds of Jesus Christ. He calls to all
weary, heavy-laden souls; consequently He calls to you. Your
coming to Him will be a proof of your election. The devils know
nothing of God's decrees. If ever Satan should tempt you so
again, say, 'If I do perish, I will perish at the feet of Christ.' He
is willing to save, to save to the uttermost. He sees, he feels
your anguish. He longs to rejoice over you. Venture therefore
upon him.

Thomas, be not faithless, but believing. Christ shall yet show
you his hands and his feet. He is the same now as He was
yesterday, full of love and graciousness to self-condemned sinners. That you may experience the full power and efficacy of
the Redeemer's blood is the ardent prayer of, dear Thomas,

Your sincere friend.

George Whitefield (1714–1770), Letter to Thomas Webb

13   Near to Death

Jesu, Maria – I am near to death,
   And Thou art calling me; I know it now.
Not by the token of this faltering breath,
   This chill at heart, this dampness on my brow, –
  (Jesu, have mercy! Mary, pray for me!)
   'Tis this new feeling, never felt before,
  (Be with me, Lord, in my extremity!)
   That I am going, that I am no more.

'Tis this strange innermost abandonment,
  (Lover of souls! great God! I look to Thee,)
This emptying out of each constituent
  And natural force, by which I come to be.
Pray for me, O my friends; a visitant
  Is knocking his dire summons at my door,
The like of whom, to scare me and to daunt,
  Has never, never come to me before;
'Tis death, – O loving friends, your prayers! – 'tis he! . . .
As though my very being had given way,
  As though I was no more a substance now,
And could fall back on nought to be my stay,
  (Help, loving Lord! Thou art my sole Refuge, Thou,)
And turn no whither, but must needs decay
  And drop from out the universal frame
Into that shapeless, scopeless, blank abyss,
  That utter nothingness, of which I came:

This is it that has come to pass in me;
Oh, horror! this it is, my dearest, this;
So pray for me, my friends, who have not strength to pray.

John Henry Newman (1801–1890), 'The Dream of Gerontius'

──────────── 14   *The Death of Arthur* ────────────

And Arthur himself wounded with a broad slaughter-spear;
fifteen dreadful wounds he had; in the least one might thrust
two gloves! Then was there no more remained in the fight, of
two hundred thousand men that there lay hewed in pieces,
except Arthur the King alone and two of his knights.

  Arthur was wounded wondrously much. There came to him
a lad, who was of his kindred; he was Cador's son, the Earl of
Cornwall; Constantine the lad hight, he was dear to the king.
Arthur looked on him, where he lay on the ground, and said
these words, with sorrowful heart: 'Constantine, thou art welcome; thou wert Cador's son. I give thee here my kingdom . . .
And I will fare to Avalun . . . to Argante the queen, and she
shall make my wounds all sound; make me all whole with

healing draughts. And afterwards I will come again to my kingdom, and dwell with the Britons with mickle joy.'

Even with the words there approached from the sea that was a short boat, floating with the waves; and two women therein, wondrously formed; and they took Arthur anon, and bare him quickly, and laid him softly down, and forth they gan depart.

Then was it accomplished that Merlin whilom said, that mickle care should be of Arthur's departure. The Britons believe yet that he is alive, and dwelleth in Avalun with the fairest of all elves; and the Britons ever yet expect when Arthur shall return. Was never the man born, of ever any lady chosen, that knoweth of the sooth, to say more of Arthur. But whilom was a sage hight Merlin; he said with words – his sayings were sooth – that an Arthur should yet come to help the English.

Layamon (c. 1200), *Brut*

───────────── 15 *A Son's Death* ─────────────

Had it pleased God to continue to me the hopes of succession, I should have been, according to my mediocrity, and the mediocrity of the age I live in, a sort of founder of a family: I should have left a son, who, in all the points in which personal merit can be viewed, in science, in erudition, in genius, in taste, in honour, in generosity, in humanity, in every liberal sentiment, and every liberal accomplishment, would not have shown himself inferior to the Duke of Bedford, or to any of those whom he traces in his line. His grace very soon would have wanted all plausibility in his attack upon that provision which belonged more to mine than to me. He would soon have supplied every deficiency, and symmetrized every disproportion. It would not have been for that successor to resort to any stagnant wasting reservoir of merit in me, or in any ancestry. He had in himself a salient, living spring of generous and manly action. Every day he lived he would have re-purchased the bounty of the crown, and ten times more, if ten times more he had received. He was made a public creature; and had no enjoyment whatever but in the performance of some duty. At this exigent moment, the loss of a finished man is not easily supplied.

But a Disposer whose power we are little able to resist and whose wisdom it behoves us not at all to dispute, has ordained it in another manner, and (whatever my querulous weakness might suggest) a far better. The storm has gone over me; and I lie like one of those old oaks which the late hurricane has scattered about me. I am stripped of all my honours, I am torn up by the roots, and lie prostrate on the earth! There, and prostrate there, I most unfeignedly recognize the Divine Justice, and in some degree submit to it . . . I greatly deceive myself, if in this hard season I would give a peck of refuse wheat for all that is called fame and honour in the world.

Edmund Burke (1729–1797), *A Letter to a Noble Lord*

16   Execution on Snow Hill

Blood demands blood. Does it? The system of compensation might be carried on ad infinitum – an eye for an eye and a tooth for a tooth, as by the old Mosaic Law. Why, because you lose your eye, is that of your opponent to be extracted? Where is the reason for the practice? Knowing that revenge is not only evil but useless we have given it up on minor points. Only to the last we stick firm. I came away from Snow Hill that morning with a disgust for murder, but it was for the murder I saw done. I pray to Almighty God to cause this disgraceful sin to pass from among us, and to cleanse our land of blood.

William Thackeray (1811–1863), 'On Going to See a Man Hanged'

17   The Death of Sydney Carton

They said of him, about the city that night, that it was the peacefullest man's face ever beheld there. Many added that he looked sublime and prophetic.

One of the most remarkable sufferers by the same axe – a woman – had asked at the foot of the same scaffold, not long before, to be allowed to write down the thoughts that were inspiring her. If he had given any utterance to his, and they were prophetic, they would have been these:

'I see . . . long ranks of the new oppressors who have risen on the destruction of the old, perishing by this retributive instrument, before it shall cease out of its present use. I see a beautiful city and a brilliant people rising from this abyss, and, in their struggles to be truly free, in their triumphs and defeats, through long long years to come, I see the evil of this time and the previous time of which this is the natural birth, gradually making expiation for itself and wearing out.

'I see the lives for which I lay down my life, peaceful, useful, prosperous and happy, in that England which I shall see no more. I see Her with a child upon her bosom, who bears my name. I see her father, aged and bent, but otherwise restored, and faithful to all men in his healing office, and at peace. I see the good old man, so long their friend, in ten years' time enriching them with all he has, and passing tranquilly to his reward.

'I see that I hold a sanctuary in their hearts, and in the hearts of their descendants, generations hence. I see her, an old woman, weeping for me on the anniversary of this day. I see her and her husband, their course done, lying side by side in their last earthly bed, and I know that each was not more honoured and held sacred in the other's soul, than I was in the souls of both.

'I see that child who lay upon her bosom and who bore my name, a man winning his way up in that path of life which once was mine. I see him winning it so well, that my name is made illustrious there by the light of his. I see the blots I threw upon it, faded away. I see him, foremost of just judges and honoured men, bringing a boy of my name, with a forehead that I know and golden hair, to this place – then fair to look upon, with not a trace of this day's disfigurement – and I hear him tell the child my story, with a tender and a faltering voice.

'It is a far, far better thing that I do, than I have ever done; it is a far, far better rest that I go to, than I have ever known.'

Charles Dickens (1812–1870), *A Tale of Two Cities*

One hundred feet from off the ground
   That noble Aloe blows;
But mark ye by what skill profound
   His charming grandeur rose.

One hundred years of patient care
   The gardners did bestow,
Toil and hereditary pray'r
   Made all this glorious show.

Thus man goes on from year to year,
   And bears no fruit at all;
But gracious God, still unsevere,
   Bids show'rs of blessings fall.

The beams of mercy, dews of grace,
   Our Saviour still supplies –
Ha! ha! the soul regains her place,
   And sweetens all the skies.

Christopher Smart (1722–1771)

————————— 19   *Phoenix* —————————

ARE you willing to be sponged out, erased, cancelled,
made nothing?
Are you willing to be made nothing?
dipped into oblivion?
If not, you will never really change.

The phoenix renews her youth
only when she is burnt, burnt alive, burnt down
to hot and flocculent ash.
Then the small stirring of a new small bub in the nest
with strands of down like floating ash
shows that she is renewing her youth like the eagle,
immortal bird.

D. H. Lawrence (1885–1930)

————— 20 *The Burden Lifting* —————

Now I saw in my dream, that the highway up which Christian
was to go, was fenced on either side with a Wall, and that
Wall is called Salvation. Up this way therefore did burdened
Christian run, but not without great difficulty, because of the
load on his back.

He ran thus till he came at a place somewhat ascending;
and upon that place stood a Cross, and a little below in the
bottom, a sepulchre. So I saw in my dream, that just as
Christian came up with the Cross, his burden loosed from
off his shoulders, and fell from off his back; and began to
tumble, and so continued to do till it came to the mouth of
the sepulchre, where it fell in, and I saw it no more.

Then was Christian glad and lightsome, and said with a
merry heart, 'He hath given me rest, by his sorrow, and life,
by his death.' Then he stood still a while, to look and wonder;
for it was very surprising to him that the sight of the Cross
should thus ease him of his burden. He looked therefore,
and looked again, even till the springs that were in his head
sent the waters down his cheeks. Now as he stood looking
and weeping, behold three Shining Ones came to him, and
saluted him, with 'Peace be to thee.' So the first said to him,
'Thy sins be forgiven.' The second stripped him of his rags,
and clothed him with a change of raiment. The third also set
a mark on his forehead, and gave him a roll with a seal upon
it, which he bid him look on as he ran, and that he should
give it in at the celestial Gate: so they went their way. Then
Christian gave three leaps for joy, and went on singing,

'Thus far did I come loaden with my sin,
Nor could aught ease the grief that I was in,
Till I came hither. What a place is this!
Must here be the beginning of my bliss?
Must here the burden fall from off my back?
Must here the strings that bound it to me, crack?
Blessed Cross! Blessed Sepulchre!
  Blessed rather be
The man that there was put to shame for me.'

John Bunyan (1628–1688), *The Pilgrim's Progress*

Hymn: When I Survey

When I survey the wondrous cross
  On which the Prince of Glory died,
My richest gain I count but loss,
  And pour contempt on all my pride.

Forbid it, Lord, that I should boast
  Save in the cross of Christ my God;
All the vain things that charm me most,
  I sacrifice them to his blood.

See from his head, his hands, his feet,
  Sorrow and love flow mingling down;
Did e'er such love and sorrow meet,
  Or thorns compose so rich a crown?

Were the whole realm of nature mine,
  That were an offering far too small;
Love so amazing, so divine,
  Demands my soul, my life, my all.

Isaac Watts (1674–1748)

Give us, O Lord God, a deep sense of Thy wonderful love towards us; how Thou wouldst not let us alone in our ruin, but didst come after us, in the Person of Thy Son Jesus Christ to bring us back to our true home with Thee.

Quicken in us, O Lord, the Spirit of gratitude, of loyalty and of sacrifice, that we may seek in all things to please Him who humbled Himself for us, even to the death of the Cross, by dying unto sin and living unto righteousness; through the same Jesus Christ our Lord.

Charles Vaughan (1816–1897)

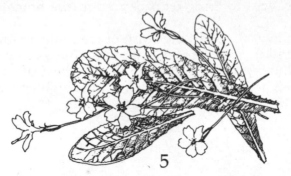

5

The Empty Tomb

Thanks be to thee, O Lord Jesus Christ, for all the benefits which thou hast given us, for all the pains and insults which thou hast borne for us. O most merciful Redeemer, Friend and Brother, may we know thee more clearly, love thee more dearly, and follow thee more nearly, now and for evermore.

Richard of Chichester (c. 1197–1253)

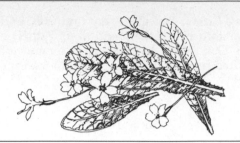

The first day of the week cometh Mary Magdalene early, when it was yet dark, unto the sepulchre, and seeth the stone taken away from the sepulchre. Then she runneth, and cometh to Simon Peter, and to the other disciple, whom Jesus loved, and saith unto them, They have taken away the Lord out of the sepulchre, and we know not where they have laid him. Peter therefore went forth, and that other disciple, and came to the sepulchre. So they ran both together: and the other disciple did outrun Peter, and came first to the sepulchre. And he stooping down, and looking in, saw the linen clothes lying; yet went he not in. Then cometh Simon Peter following him, and went into the sepulchre, and seeth the linen clothes lie, and the napkin, that was about his head, not lying with the linen clothes, but wrapped together in a place by itself. Then went in also that other disciple, which came first to the sepulchre, and he saw, and believed. For as yet they knew not the Scripture, that he must rise again from the dead. Then the disciples went away again unto their own home.

But Mary stood without at the sepulchre weeping: and as she wept, she stooped down, and looked into the sepulchre, and seeth two angels in white sitting, the one at the head, and the other at the feet, where the body of Jesus had lain. And they say unto her, Woman, why weepest thou? She saith unto them, Because they have taken away my Lord, and I know not where they have laid him.

And when she had thus said, she turned herself back, and saw Jesus standing, and knew not that it was Jesus. Jesus saith unto her, Woman, why weepest thou? whom seekest thou? She, supposing him to be the gardener, saith unto him, Sir, if thou have borne him hence, tell me where thou hast laid him, and I will take him away. Jesus saith unto her, Mary. She turned herself, and saith unto him, Rabboni; which is to say, Master. Jesus saith unto her, Touch me not; for I am not yet ascended to my Father: but go to my brethren, and say unto them, I ascend unto my Father, and your Father; and to my God, and your God. Mary Magdalene came and told the disciples that she had seen the Lord, and that he had spoken these things unto her.

John 20:1–18

1   New Life

The very notion 'resurrection' needs to be clarified before we discuss the implications. In one sense, it refers to what happened once with Jesus when he passed through death to the new, risen life . . . a foretaste of the glorious future awaiting us in the completion of God's plan. This is the prime meaning, for it is from this aspect that the others derive. The second meaning appears when it is applied to Baptism, and we speak with the apostle of going down in the waters of baptism to death and rising again in the new life. And then there is a third meaning, which can happen, and happen more than once, in the life of each and any individual. This is the resurrection which comes to the individual, waking him or her to the surrounding world in an entirely new way; it is like a sudden break and leap forward in our personal evolution.

Michael Hollings (b. 1921), *I Will be There*

2   Easter Day

Most glorious Lord of life, that on this day,
  Didst make Thy triumph over death and sin:
  And having harrow'd hell, didst bring away
  Captivity thence captive, us to win:
This joyous day, dear Lord, with joy begin,
  And grant that we for whom Thou diddest die
  Being with Thy dear blood clean wash'd from sin,
  May live for ever in felicity.
And that Thy love we weighing worthily,
  May likewise love Thee for the same again:
  And for Thy sake that all like dear didst buy,
  With love may one another entertain.
So let us love, dear love, like as we ought,
  Love is the lesson which the Lord us taught.

Edmund Spenser (c. 1552–1599)

3 Christ's Love-Song

Love me brought,
And love me wrought,
  Man, to be thy fere.
Love me fed,
And love me led
  And love me lettet here.

Love me slew,
And love me drew,
  And love me laid on bier.
Love is my peace;
For love I chese,
  Man to buyen dear.

Ne dread thee nought,
I have thee sought,
  Bothen day and night,
To haven thee
Well is me,
  I have thee won in fight.

Anonymous (Medieval)

4 Jesus Greeting His Mother

Then the creature was left still with Our Lady and thought it a
thousand years till the third day came; and that day, she was
with Our Lady in a chapel where Our Lord Jesus Christ
appeared unto her, and said:
  'Greetings, holy parent.'
  And then the creature thought, in her soul, that Our Lady
said:

'Thou art my sweet Son, Jesus?'

And He said:

'Yea, blessed Mother, I am your own Son, Jesus.'

Then He took up His blessed Mother and kissed her fully sweetly.

And then the creature thought that she saw Our Lady feeling and tasting Our Lord's Body all over, and His hands and His feet, to see if there was any soreness or any pain. And she heard Our Lord say to His Mother:

'Dear Mother, My pain is all gone, and now shall I live for evermore. And Mother, so shall your pain and your sorrow be turned into full great joy. Mother, ask what ye will, and I shall tell you.'

And when He had suffered His Mother to ask what she would, and had answered to her questions, then He said:

'Mother, by your leave, I must go and speak with Mary Magdalene.'

Our Lady said: 'It is well done, for, Son, she hath full much sorrow for Your absence. And I pray You, be not long from me.'

These ghostly sights and understandings caused the creature to weep, to sob, and to cry full loud, so that she might not control herself or restrain herself there-from, on Easter Day and other days, when Our Lord would visit her with His grace, blessed and worshipped may He be.

And anon afterwards, the creature was, in her contemplation, with Mary Magdalene, mourning and seeking Our Lord at the grave, and heard and saw how Our Lord Jesus Christ appeared to her in the likeness of a gardener, saying:

'Woman, why weepest thou?'

Mary, not knowing who He was, all inflamed with the fire of love, answered Him:

'Sir, if thou hast taken away my Lord, tell me, and I shall take Him back again.'

Our Merciful Lord, having pity and compassion on her, said:

'Mary.'

With that word, she, knowing Our Lord, fell down at His feet, and would have kissed His feet, saying:

'Master.'

Our Lord said to her: 'Touch Me not.'

Then the creature thought that Mary Magdalene said to Our Lord:

'Ah! Lord, I see well Ye will not that I be so homely with You as I have been before,' and made a grieving look.

'Yes, Mary,' said Our Lord, 'I shall never forsake thee, but I shall ever be with thee without end.'

And then Our Lord said to Mary Magdalene:

'Go! Tell My brethren and Peter that I am up-risen.'

And then the creature thought that Mary went forth with great joy, and it was great marvel to her that Mary rejoiced, for if Our Lord had spoken to her as He did to Mary, she thought that she could never have been merry. That was when she would have kissed His feet, and He said: 'Touch Me not.'

The creature had such great grief and misery in that word that, whenever she heard it in any sermon, as she did many times, she wept, sorrowed and cried, as if she would have died, for the love and desire that she had to be with Our Lord.

Margery Kempe (c. 1373–1439), *The Book of Margery Kempe*

───── 5 *The Source of Redemption* ─────

We are told . . . of the *source* of our redemption – the love of God for a lost world; *who* the Redeemer is – the Son of God; and the *purpose* for which this plan was formed and executed – 'That whosoever believed in him should not perish but have everlasting life.' There is nothing surely in all this to promote gloominess. If kindness and mercy have a tendency to win and warm the heart, here is every incentive to joy and cheerfulness. Christianity looks kindly upon everyone, and with peculiar tenderness on those who, from humbling views of their own unworthiness, might be led to imagine themselves excluded. We are expressly told that 'Christ died for *all*'; that 'He tasted death for *every* man'; that 'He died for the sins of the *whole* world.' Accordingly, He has commanded that His Gospel should be preached 'to *every* creature', which is, in effect, declaring that not a single human being is excluded. To preach the Gospel is to offer a Saviour, and the Saviour in the plainest language offers Himself to all, declaring 'to all the ends of the earth': 'Look unto me and be saved.' It is therefore an undeniable truth that no one will perish for lack of a Saviour, but by rejecting Him . . .

We may see how suitable is redemption in Christ to a fallen

man! How exactly it meets every need! No one needs now perish because he is a sinner, provided he is willing to forsake his sin, for 'Jesus Christ came into the world to save sinners' and 'He is now exalted to be a prince and a Saviour, to give repentance and forgiveness of sin.' This passage, let us observe, points out to us the order in which He bestows His blessings: He *first* gives repentance, and *then* forgiveness.

Hannah More (1745–1833), *Strictures on the Modern System of Female Education*

─── 6　*The Bridegroom and His Bride* ───

For he is risen from death t' eternal life,
And now those precious ointments he desires
Are brought unto him, by his faithful wife
The holy Church; who in those rich attires,
Of patience, love, long-suffering, void of strife,
Humbly presents those ointments he requires:
　　The oils of mercy, charity, and faith,
　　She only gives that which no other hath.

These precious balms do heal his grievous wounds,
And water of compunction washeth clean
The sores of sins, which in our souls abound;
So fair it heals, no scar is ever seen;
Yet all the glory unto Christ redounds,
His precious blood is that which must redeem;
　　Those well may make us lovely in his sight,
　　But cannot save without his powerful might.

This is that bridegroom that appears so fair,
So sweet, so lovely in his spouse's sight,
That unto snow we may his face compare,
His cheeks like scarlet, and his eyes so bright
As purest doves that in the rivers are,
Washed with milk, to give the more delight;
　　His head is likened to the finest gold,
　　His curled locks so beauteous to behold;

Black as a raven in her blackest hue;
His lips like scarlet threads, yet much more sweet
Than is the sweetest honey dropping dew,
Or honeycombs, where all the bees do meet;
Yea, he is constant, and his words are true,
His cheeks are beds of spices, flowers sweet;
 His lips like lilies, dropping down pure myrrh,
 Whose love, before all worlds we do prefer.

Emelia Lanyer (1569–1645), 'Salve Deus Rex Iudaeorum'

———— 7 *That Unique Combination* ————

I was so glad to get your first Old Rectory letter of 30 March.
But first let me say that I have purposely waited till we should
have got through these every year newly wonderful Church
days – so as to be able to refer to the entire prism of many-
coloured fact and emotion – which only thus together give us
the true Christian reality and life. The great fact, and even the
commemoration of, Good Friday, would, alone, be too austere,
too heartbreaking; the great fact, and even just the feast of
Easter, if alone – even if they had followed upon Our Lord's
Hidden Life, or even His Preaching, but without the Passion
and its commemoration, would not have drained the Cup – the
bitter Cup – of the possibilities of earthly human life and earthly
human interconnection to the dregs. Good Friday *and* Easter
Sunday, the two together, each requiring the other, and we all
requiring both – only this twin fact gives us Christianity, where
suffering holds a necessary place, but never the place of the
end, always only of the means. My great Troeltsch always
marvels anew at that *unique* combination effected by Christianity
– so earnest and so *un*rigoristic – so expansive and so full of
suffering without morbidness, and of joy without sentimen-
tality. We will all, please God, see this more and more every
year, that these bitter-sweet, contraction-expansion, sacrifice-
serenity, great days come round.

Friedrich Von Hügel (1852–1925), Letter to his niece

8 No Flaming Lustre

It is no flaming lustre made of light,
No sweet consent or well-timed harmony,
Ambrosia for to feast the appetite,
Or flowery odour mixed with spicery,
No soft embrace or pleasure bodily;
   And yet it is a kind of inward feast,
   A harmony that sounds within the breast,
An odour, light, embrace, in which the soul doth rest,

A heavenly feast no hunger can consume,
A light unseen, yet shines in every place,
A sound no time can steal, a sweet perfume
No winds can scatter, an entire embrace
That no satiety can e'er unlace.
   Ingraced into so high a favour there,
   The saints with their beau-peers whole worlds outwear,
And things unseen do see, and things unheard do hear.

Giles Fletcher (c. 1584–1623), 'The Celestial City'

9 New Light, New Roads

If my mind can't quite take certain things – such as the physical
Resurrection – does it matter, so long as it doesn't get in the
way of belief in Christ as master and saviour and helper, to be
sought and served? I know it mattered to the early church, and
was perhaps the only way in which they could be convinced –
but should one try to force or persuade one's mind to it, if one
feels one doesn't need it? You say 'we cannot be expected to
do more than yield to God the minds which we actually possess', so I suppose God takes them and does what he can with
them. And of course in time they might develop new powers
of faith; as you say, it depends on what happens to make
connections. He keeps showing us new things, new light on

the past, new roads for the future, and one hopes for new powers. But what moors, fens, crags and torrents lie all about.

Rose Macaulay (1881–1958), Letter to a friend

────────── *10 Infinite and Eternal* ──────────

In writing in this way about Jesus we must not distort the fact that he was a man, born of human parents. He undoubtedly made a tremendous impact on many people, some of whom found relief from physical illness as a result of their trust in him. In their desire to emphasise his supreme value to them, some of his followers in later years described his life and activities in miraculous terms. Whether we accept this explanation is not important; what matters is the greatness of his personality and his spiritual insight. Because his teaching and way of life ran counter to the convictions and practices of the religious leaders of his time, they, with the consent of the populace, engineered his trial and execution. Men do not like goodness if it challenges their moral failure, or loyalty to truth that calls for a revolutionary change of mind. They killed Jesus because they were afraid of him.

As in his life, so in his approach to death Jesus never faltered in his trust in love, and forgave those who rejected him. By this creative attitude Jesus radically changed a most heinous act of human wickedness into an event that has released love and forgiveness into a dark world. For ever after people know that such love can overcome evil, and in this knowledge have found freedom to live.

Many Friends are sceptical about the New Testament accounts of the physical resurrection of Jesus, although for some this is a crucial element in their faith. Most would agree that the essential meaning behind the story of the first Easter is that death could not destroy all that was of real value in the earthly life of Jesus. The love experienced by his disciples could not be taken from them by his death, because they recognized that it was of an infinite and eternal quality. In fact, it was only after his death that they came to understand and to appreciate fully the deep meaning of his life and to be set free by it.

George H. Gorman (1916–1982), *Introducing Quakers*

11 Easter Night

All night had shout of men and cry
  Of woeful women filled his way;
Until that noon of sombre sky
  On Friday, clamour and display
Smote him; no solitude had he,
No silence, since Gethsemane.

Public was Death; but Power, but Might,
  But Life again, but Victory,
Were hushed within the dead of night,
  The shuttered dark, the secrecy.
And all alone, alone, alone,
He rose again behind the stone.

Alice Meynell (1849–1922)

12 Melted and New-fashioned

If an old silver goblet be melted, and new-fashioned after a beautiful manner, then is it better than afore, and neither spilt nor destroyed. Even so have we no just cause to complain of death, whereby the body being delivered from all filthiness, shall in his due time be perfectly renewed.

The egg shell, though it be goodly and fair-fashioned, must be opened and broken, that the young chick may slip out of it. None otherwise doth death dissolve and break up our body, but to the intent that we may attain to the life of heaven.

The mother's womb carrieth the child seven or nine months, and prepareth it, not for itself, but for the world wherein we are born. Even so this present time over all upon earth serveth not to this end, that we must ever be here, but that we should be brought forth and born out of the body of the world into another and everlasting life. Hereunto behold the words of Christ: *A woman, when she travaileth, hath sorrow because her hour is come: but as soon as she is delivered of the child, she remembereth no more the anguish, for joy that a man is born into the world.* Namely, like as a child out of the small habitation of his mother's womb, with danger and anguish is born into this wide world; even so goeth a man through the narrow gate of death with distress and trouble out of the earth into the heavenly life. For this cause did the old Christians call the death of the saints a new birth. Therefore ought we to note well this comfort, that to die is not to perish, but to be first of all born aright.

Miles Coverdale (c. 1488–1569), 'How a Christian man ought to behave himself in the danger of death'

13 A Pure Flame

A great part of antiquity contented their hopes of subsistency with a transmigration of their souls: a good way to continue their memories, while, having the advantage of plural successions, they could not but act something remarkable in such variety of beings, and, enjoying the fame of their past selves, make accumulation of glory unto their last durations. Others, rather than be lost in the uncomfortable night of nothing, were content to recede into the common being, and make one particle of the public soul of all things – which was no more than to return into their unknown and divine original again . . .

There is nothing strictly immortal but immortality: whatever hath no beginning may be confident of no end. All others have a dependent being, and within the reach of destruction; which is the peculiar of that necessary essence that cannot destroy itself, and the highest strain of omnipotency, to be so powerfully constituted as not to suffer even from the power of itself. But the sufficiency of Christian immortality frustrates all earthly glory, and the quality of either state after death, makes a folly of posthumous memory. God, who can only destroy our souls, and hath assured our resurrection, either of our bodies or names hath directly promised no duration . . .

Life is a pure flame, and we live by an invisible sun within us. A small fire sufficeth for life: great flames seemed too little after death.

Thomas Browne (1605–1682), *Hydriotaphia*

14 The Tombs of the Great

For my own part, though I am always serious, I do not know
what it is to be melancholy; and can therefore take a view of
nature in her deep and solemn scenes, with the same pleasure
as in her most gay and delightful ones. By this means I can
improve my self with those objects, which others consider with
terror. When I look upon the tombs of the great, every emotion
of envy dies in me; when I read the epitaphs of the beautiful,
every inordinate desire goes out; when I meet with the grief of
parents upon a tomb-stone, my heart melts with compassion;
when I see the tomb of the parents themselves, I consider the
vanity of grieving for those whom we must quickly follow.
When I see kings lying by those who deposed them, when I
consider rival wits placed side by side, or the holy men that
divided the world with their contests and disputes, I reflect
with sorrow and astonishment on the little competitions, fac-
tions, and debates of mankind. When I read the several dates
of the tombs of some that died yesterday, and some six hundred
years ago, I consider that great day when we shall all of us be
contemporaries, and make our appearance together.

Joseph Addison (1672–1719), 'The Tombs in Westminster
Abbey'

15 Where the Cows Lay

Being so often – possibly not always by chance – the first two
persons to get up at the dairy-house, they seemed to themselves
the first persons up of all the world. In these early days of her
residence here Tess did not skim, but went out of doors at once
after rising, where he was generally awaiting her. The spectral,
half-compounded, aqueous light which pervaded the open
mead, impressed them with a feeling of isolation, as if they
were Adam and Eve. At this dim inceptive stage of the day
Tess seemed to Clare to exhibit a dignified largeness both of
disposition and physique, an almost regnant power, possibly
because he knew that at that preternatural time hardly any

woman so well endowed in person as she was likely to be walking in the open air within the boundaries of his horizon; very few in all England. Fair women are usually asleep at midsummer dawns. She was close at hand, and the rest were nowhere.

The mixed, singular, luminous gloom in which they walked along together to the spot where the cows lay, often made him think of the Resurrection hour. He little thought that the Magdalen might be at his side. Whilst all the landscape was in neutral shade his companion's face, which was the focus of his eyes, rising above the mist stratum, seemed to have a sort of phosphorescence upon it. She looked ghostly, as if she were merely a soul at large. In reality her face, without appearing to do so, had caught the cold gleam of day from the north-east; his own face, though he did not think of it, wore the same aspect to her.

Thomas Hardy (1840–1928), *Tess of the d'Urbervilles*

─────────── *16 Beyond the Dark Gate* ───────────

There was not much of a dawn; but enough. A shaft of sunlight, brief but real, broke through at about six o'clock. Several voices shouted excitedly at the sight, and a boy ran to the castle gateway, stooped over the swathe of white cloth still lying there, and then, standing, he tossed what looked like a golden quoit high into the air. It shone as it soared through the early sunshine and all the Resurrection was in it. Then another boy standing on the top of the gate tower caught it and made it fast, and I saw now that there was twine attached to it. Up came the white swathe, pulled from above, and fell open, floating on the breeze, like a great flag or a great kite. We all saw now that it was of some semi-transparent, shimmering stuff, and it was cut into shapes which moved over each other and cast wonderful shadows. There it floated and flew, clothing the gate tower as though the castle itself had risen with a new and glorified body.

While that lovely thing danced in the sun, which came and went with shafts and sudden shadows, the inhabitants of the castle were of course dancing below it, a dance of the Risen Life, with leaps, springs and cartwheels over one another. They must have been as tired as we, the guests, certainly were, but none of us was feeling it yet; how could we? Then at last the Eucharist was celebrated on a new altar in the castle hall, and truly I felt as though I had lived through all paganism before we reached it. The changing sunlight fell on the old stones of the hall and on Jill and me as we knelt there. I felt limp and at peace, drained and purged to the bottom of my being, many depths further down than I could see into myself.

I don't think the danced liturgies were finished even now, but I had to go, so as to spend part at least of the holiday at home. As we drove away, I looked back and saw the white flag of the risen body shining above and the empty gateway beneath. The story was not finished yet. Suddenly I wondered, and wonder still, what strange salvation was indeed taking place beyond the dark gate of my dreams.

Caroline Glyn (1947–1981), *A Mountain at the End of Night*

17 Glory Be

'Hush!' said the Cabby. They all listened.

In the darkness something was happening at last. A voice had begun to sing. It was very far away and Digory found it hard to decide from what direction it was coming. Sometimes it seemed to come from all directions at once. Sometimes he almost thought it was coming out of the earth beneath them. Its lower notes were deep enough to be the voice of the earth itself. There were no words. There was hardly even a tune. But it was, beyond comparison, the most beautiful noise he had ever heard. It was so beautiful he could hardly bear it. The horse seemed to like it too: he gave the sort of whinny a horse would give if, after years of being a cab-horse, it found itself back in the old field where it had played as a foal, and saw someone whom it remembered and loved coming across the field to bring it a lump of sugar.

'Gawd!' said the Cabby. 'Ain't it lovely?'

Then two wonders happened at the same moment. One was that the voice was suddenly joined by other voices; more voices than you could possibly count. They were in harmony with it, but far higher up the scale: cold, tingling, silvery voices. The second wonder was that the blackness overhead, all at once, was blazing with stars. They didn't come out gently one by one, as they do on a summer evening. One moment there had been nothing but darkness; next moment a thousand, thousand points of light leaped out – single stars, constellations, and planets, brighter and bigger than any in our world. There were no clouds. The new stars and the new voices began at exactly the same time. If you had seen and heard it, as Digory did, you would have felt quite certain that it was the stars themselves which were singing, and that it was the First Voice, the deep one, which had made them appear and made them sing.

'Glory be!' said the Cabby, 'I'd ha' been a better man all my life if I'd known there were things like this.'

C. S. Lewis (1898–1963), *The Magician's Nephew*

18   The Choir Invisible

O may I join the choir invisible
Of those immortal dead who live again
In minds made better by their presence: live
In pulses stirred to generosity,
In deeds of daring rectitude, in scorn
For miserable aims that end with self,
In thoughts sublime that pierce the night like stars,
And with their mild persistence urge man's search
To vaster issues . . .
                      This is the life to come,
Which martyred men have made more glorious
For us who strive to follow. May I reach
That purest heaven, be to other souls
The cup of strength in some great agony,
Enkindle generous ardour, feed pure love,
Beget the smiles that have no cruelty –
Be the sweet presence of a good diffused,
And in diffusion ever more intense.
So shall I join the choir invisible
Whose music is the gladness of the world.

George Eliot (1819–1880)

The happiest, brightest, most beautiful Easter I have ever spent. I woke early and looked out. As I had hoped the day was cloudless, a glorious morning. My first thought was 'Christ is Risen'. It is not well to lie in bed on Easter morning, indeed it is thought very unlucky. I got up between five and six and was out soon after six. There had been a frost and the air was rimy with a heavy thick white dew on hedge, bank and turf, but the morning was not cold. There was a heavy white dew with a touch of hoar frost on the meadows, and as I leaned over the wicket gate by the mill pond looking to see if there were any primroses in the banks but not liking to venture into the dripping grass suddenly I heard the cuckoo for the first time this year. He was near Peter's Pool and he called three times quickly one after another. It is very well to hear the cuckoo for the first time on Easter Sunday morning. I loitered up the lane again gathering primroses.

The village lay quiet and peaceful in the morning sunshine, but by the time I came back from primrosing there was some little stir and people were beginning to open their doors and look out into the fresh fragrant splendid morning.

There was a very large congregation at morning church, the largest I have seen for some time, attracted by Easter and the splendour of the day, for they have here an immense reverence for Easter Sunday. The anthem went very well and Mr. Baskerville complimented Mr. Evans after church about it, saying that it was sung in good tune and time and had been a great treat. There were more communicants than usual: 29. This is the fifth time I have received the Sacrament within four days. After morning service I took Mr. V. round the churchyard and showed him the crosses on his mother's, wife's, and brother's graves. He was quite taken by surprise and very much gratified. I am glad to see that our primrose crosses seem to be having some effect for I think I notice this Easter some attempt to copy them and an advance towards the form of the cross in some of the decorations of the graves. I wish we could get the people to adopt some little design in the disposition of the flowers upon the graves instead of sticking sprigs into the turf aimlessly anywhere, anyhow and with no meaning at all. But one does not like to interfere too much with their artless, natural way of showing their respect and love for the dead. I am thankful to find this beautiful custom on the increase, and observed more and more every year. Some years ago it was on the decline and nearly discontinued. On Easter Day all the young people come out in something new and bright like butterflies. It is almost part of their religion to wear something new on this day. It was an old saying that if you don't wear something new on Easter Day, the crows will spoil everything you have on.

Between the services a great many people were in the church-yard looking at the graves. I went to Bettws Chapel in the afternoon. It was burning hot and as I climbed the hill the perspiration rolled off my forehead from under my hat and fell in drops on the dusty road. Lucretia Wall was in chapel looking pale and pretty after her illness. Coming down the hill it was delightful, cool and pleasant. The sweet suspicion of spring strengthens, deepens, and grows more sweet every day. Mrs. Pring gave us lamb and asparagus at dinner.

Francis Kilvert (1840–1879), *Kilvert's Diary*

──────── *20 Beautiful for Thee* ────────

The weather's gettin' springy,
An' the birds are gettin' singy.
And it would not do to let the cadets know what a longing I have just now to be away from the Training College.
Away, away from men and towns
To the wild wood and the downs!
Can you understand the feeling? It came over me a few days ago with a rush. Suddenly I knew the spring had come. I knew the buds were bursting. I knew the little streams in the meadows were hurrying with cheerful swiftness about their business, singing as they went. The very wind, I felt sure, would be dropping its rough ways and starting already to prac-tise the refreshing and caressing touch that will be all the fashion when it is greeting the delicate new blossoms that will presently make the humpy old fruit trees look like fairies.

And I find myself – the human part of me – hankering after long, long tramps over the common, or by the sea, or through the lanes – anywhere where the smell and the song and the sunshine of the spring will be around me, so that the inspiration of it might sink into my heart and awaken in my spirit a stirring and a moving that will show itself in fresh expressions of the life of my spirit towards God . . .

May the life of Jesus be in you – in me. Then there will be new beginnings, fresh ventures, and more of all that belongs to the Divine. For in the spiritual world, as in the world of nature, the law of life is the law of growth, and the life of God in us must mean that we 'grow up into Him in all things'. His life in all that we are, the seen and the unseen; coming into everything that is a part of us, as the sap flows into everything that is a part of the tree – our thoughts, our words, our deeds. This will mean a renewing and reviving, an increasing and keeping alive the spiritual qualities of faith, love, humility, patience, self-sacrifice, forgiveness, mercy, justice, and truth.

Let us both go on thinking over what the twigs have said, and let us be more daring to make beginnings in some matters, and more trustful as to results: remembering always, even if last time we made the attempt things did not work out as we hoped – at least, perhaps, it did not seem so – it is our privilege to begin again with the spring. We shall meet discouragement in varying forms. The new beginning, the patient working out and working on, is not easy always, 'but God giveth the increase', and that makes every effort worthwhile.

Yes, dear G—, this is the message of the spring to my soul and to yours, 'God giveth the increase'; and so by faith we may claim from Him all the increase of whatever Divine quality we need, to make all that is ours show forth the beauty of His work in us; just as the trees and the grasses are showing forth the perfect grace of His work in them. 'That henceforth our lives may be – beautiful for Thee.'

Catherine Bramwell-Booth (1883–1988), Letter to G

——— *Hymn: Christ the Lord is Risen* ———

Christ the Lord is risen today;
   Alleluia!
Sons of men and angels say:
Raise your joys and triumphs high;
Sing, ye heavens; thou earth, reply:

Love's redeeming work is done,
Fought the fight, the battle won;
Vain the stone, the watch, the seal;
Christ hath burst the gates of hell:

Lives again our glorious King;
Where, O death, is now thy sting?
Once he died our souls to save;
Where's thy victory, boasting grave?

Soar we now where Christ hath led,
Following our exalted Head;
Made like him, like him we rise;
Ours the cross, the grave, the skies:

King of Glory! Soul of bliss!
Everlasting life is this,
Thee to know, thy power to prove,
Thus to sing, and thus to love:

Charles Wesley (1707–1788)

O Lord, who by triumphing over the power of darkness prepared our place in the New Jerusalem; grant us, who have this day given thanks for your resurrection, to praise you in that city of which you are the light; where with the Father and the Holy Spirit you live and reign, now and for ever.

William Bright (1824–1901)

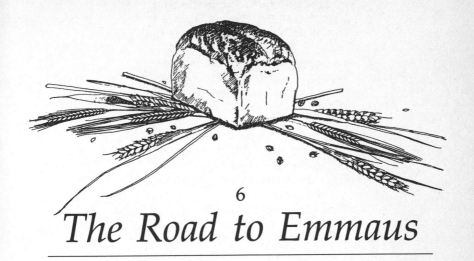

6

The Road to Emmaus

Make our hearts to burn within us, O Christ, as we walk with thee in the way and listen to thy words; that we may go in the strength of thy presence and thy truth all our journey through, and at its end behold thee, in the glory of the eternal Trinity, God for ever and ever.

Eric Milner-White (1884–1963)

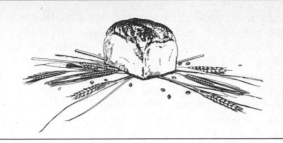

And, behold, two of them went that same day to a village called Emmaus, which was from Jerusalem about three-score furlongs. And they talked together of all these things which had happened. And it came to pass, that, while they communed together and reasoned, Jesus himself drew near, and went with them. But their eyes were holden that they should not know him.

And he said unto them, What manner of communications are these that ye have one to another, as ye walk, and are sad? And the one of them, whose name was Cleopas, answering said unto him, Art thou only a stranger in Jerusalem, and hast not known the things which are come to pass there in these days? And he said unto them, What things? And they said unto him, Concerning Jesus of Nazareth, which was a prophet mighty in deed and word before God and all the people: and how the chief priests and our rulers delivered him to be condemned to death, and have crucified him. But we trusted that it had been he which should have redeemed Israel: and beside all this, today is the third day since these things were done. Yea, and certain women also of our company made us astonished, which were early at the sepulchre; and when they found not his body, they came, saying, that they had also seen a vision of angels, which said that he was alive. And certain of them which were with us went to the sepulchre, and found it even so as the women had said: but him they saw not.

Then he said unto them, O fools, and slow of heart to believe all that the prophets have spoken: ought not Christ to have suffered these things, and to enter into his glory? And beginning at Moses and all the prophets, he expounded unto them in all the Scriptures the things concerning himself. And they drew nigh unto the village, whither they went: and he made as though he would have gone further. But they constrained him, saying, Abide with us; for it is toward evening, and the day is far spent. And he went in to tarry with them.

And it came to pass, as he sat at meat with them, he took bread, and blessed it, and brake, and gave to them. And their eyes were opened, and they knew him; and he vanished out of their sight. And they said one to another, Did not our heart burn within us, while he talked with us by the way, and while he opened to us the Scriptures?

And they rose up the same hour, and returned to Jerusalem, and found the eleven gathered together, and them that were with them, saying, The Lord is risen indeed, and hath appeared to Simon. And they told what things were done in the way, and how he was known of them in breaking of bread.

Luke 24: 13–35

1   The Sparrow's Flight

If we compare the present life of man on earth with that time which is unknown to us, it seems to me that it is like the swift flight of a sparrow through the hall where we sit at supper in the winter-time. In our midst is a warm fire, while outside storms of rain or snow are raging. The sparrow, flying in through one door and almost immediately out by another, is momentarily safe from the wintry storm, finding comfort and calm within; but then quickly it vanishes from our sight, returning to the dark winter from whence it came. Similarly our life on earth is only a brief interlude: we know nothing of what came before or of what is to come. If, therefore, this new teaching contains something more certain, it deserves our following.

Bede (673–735), *Ecclesiastical History*

2   That Face of Beauty

I seek that face of beauty past belief;
Only immortal love can ease my grief;
To see him, or to know him, ends all pain,
Turns mourning song to brightest glad refrain.

They live in joy who love that sweetest Child:
Jesu it is, of all most meek and mild.
Though sinful, one who loves him shall not fear;
Evil and wrath of God shall not come near.

I love to speak of him whose sweetness charms
My heart till it must burst, and cures all harms;
Whose unforgettable love snares all my thought,
Whose bleeding hands and feet my soul have bought.

My heart, beholding him, breaks with desire.
Fair is the love that keeps its sacred fire,
That strengthens grace though robbing us of rest:
Of all things on the earth this love is best.

No wonder I lament the gallows-tree,
Where Christ was nailed and beaten wickedly.
Heart aches to ponder on his tender cries:
Leave sin, O Man, who prompts such sacrifice.

Love's sweetness is beyond man's power to tell;
Who loves with longing, God protects from hell.
O endless joy, that those who dwell in love
Shall from their foes be saved by God above!

Jesu, who makes the day from darkness spring,
Guard us, for we acknowledge you as King.
O everlasting love whom we adore,
Give us grace to love you evermore!

Richard Rolle (c. 1300–1349), 'Love made firm in Christ'

3 · The Calling of Man

The calling of man is that natural mode of renovation whereby God the Father, according to his purpose in Christ, invites fallen man to a knowledge of the way in which he is to be propitiated and served. This calling is either general or special. The general calling is that whereby God invites the whole of mankind, in various ways, but all of them sufficient for the purpose, to the knowledge of the true Deity. God's special calling is that whereby he, at the time which he thinks proper, invites particular individuals, elect as well as reprobate, more frequently, and with a more marked call than others.

The change which takes place in man by reason of his calling, is that whereby the natural mind and will of man, being partially renewed by a divine impulse, are led to seek the knowledge of God, and, for the time being at least, undergo an alteration for the better. Inasmuch as this change is from God, those in whom it takes place are said to be enlightened, and to be endued with power to will what is good.

John Milton (1608–1674), *Christian Doctrine*

4 The Immense Ocean

Consider first, that although the Kingdom of heaven abounds with all that can be imagined good and delightful; yet there is but one sovereign good, in the enjoyment of which consists the essential beatitude of heaven, and that is God himself, whom the blessed ever see as he truly is, face to face; and see him in the very centre of their own souls; and by the eternal contemplation of his infinite beauty and truth, together with all his divine attributes and attractions, they are quite ravished, and set on fire with seraphic flames of eternal love. By means of this contemplation and love they are closely united by a most pure and amiable union, with this sovereign and infinite good, and they eternally enjoy him. He surrounds and penetrates them on all sides with inexpressible delights; he fills their whole souls with himself, the overflowing source of all good; he gives himself to them to be their joy, their treasure, their never-ending bliss; he transforms them in a manner to himself, as when brass or iron in the furnace is perfectly penetrated by fire it loseth in a manner its own nature, and becomes all flame and fire. O happy creatures! What can be wanting to complete your joys, who have within, and without you, the immense ocean of endless felicity?

Richard Challoner (1691–1781), *Meditations for Every Day in the Year*

5 Eternal Life Now

Jesus did not promise to men simply life after death, but a quality of life now. He promised us eternal life, the sharing of God's life, participation in his own risen life. He said that he had come to give men abundant life – sufficient to keep the body in health and strength, to illuminate and guide the mind, to bring peace to the heart. If we have that life within us now, we shall not worry about our last migration into the spiritual world, for we shall know a good deal about it already . . .

Eternal life is not just everlasting life, a continuation of what goes on at present, for that might not be too joyful for many people. It is a quality of life, the kind of life which Jesus had, human life permeated by the grace and love of God, and so invulnerable to physical death. Jesus taught his disciples that they could have eternal life now, just as in the teaching of the Buddha the sphere of bliss and blessing which he called Nirvana can be enjoyed now. The perfection of both will come in the dimension beyond death.

George Appleton (b. 1902), *Journey for a Soul*

6   *Waiting for You*

Death is nothing at all . . . I have only slipped away into the next room. I am I and you are you. Whatever we were to each other that we are still. Call me by my old familiar name, speak to me in the easy way which you always used. Put no difference in your tone; wear no forced air of solemnity or sorrow. Laugh as we always laughed at the little jokes we enjoyed together. Play, smile, think of me, pray for me. Let my name be ever the household word that it always was. Let it be spoken without effort, without the ghost of a shadow on it. Life means all that it ever meant. It is the same as it ever was; there is absolutely unbroken continuity. Why should I be out of mind because I am out of sight? I am waiting for you for an interval, somewhere very near, just around the corner. All is well.

Henry Scott Holland (1847–1918), attributed

7   *Ever Nigh*

Thy voice is on the rolling air;
  I hear thee where the waters run;
  Thou standest in the rising sun,
And in the setting thou art fair.

What art thou then? I cannot guess;
  But though I seem in star and flower
  To feel thee some diffusive power,
I do not therefore love thee less:

My love involves the love before;
  My love is vaster passion now;
  Though mixed with God and Nature thou,
I seem to love thee more and more.

Far off thou art, but ever nigh;
  I have thee still, and I rejoice;
  I prosper, circled with thy voice;
I shall not lose thee though I die.

Alfred Tennyson (1809–1892), 'In Memoriam'

———— 8 *Moments of Recognition* ————

Now if it is these moments of recognition and awareness that
change our minds and change our lives, if these can be the true
turning points of human history, then something of enormous
power must be at work in such commonplace experiences. One
might say that a flash of recognition has a higher voltage than
a flash of lightning, that the power that makes us suddenly
aware is the secret of all evolution and the spark that sets off
most revolutions.

But what is this force which causes me to see in a way in
which I have not seen? What makes a landscape or a person or
an idea come to life for me and become a presence towards
which I surrender myself? I recognize, I respond, I fall in love,
I worship – yet it was not I who took the first step. In every
such encounter there has been an anonymous third party who
makes the introduction, acts as a go-between, makes two beings
aware of each other, sets up a current of communication
between them. What is more, this invisible go-between does
not simply stand between us but is activating each of us from
inside.

John V. Taylor (b. 1914), *The Go-Between God*

9 Catching Glimpses

It is only in exceptional moods that we realise how wonderful are the commonest experiences of life. It seems to me sometimes that these experiences have an 'inner' side, as well as the outer side we normally perceive. At such moments one suddenly sees everything with new eyes; one feels on the brink of some great revelation. It is as if we caught a glimpse of some incredibly beautiful world that lies silently about us all the time. I remember vividly my first experience of the kind when, as a boy, I came suddenly upon the quiet miracle of an ivy-clad wall glistening under a London street-lamp. I wanted to weep and I wanted to pray; to weep for the Paradise from which I had been exiled, and to pray that I might yet be made worthy of it. Such moments are rare, in my experience. But their influence is permanent. They import a tinge of unreality into our normal acceptances; we suspect them for the dull and purblind things that they are. There are analogous moments when one suddenly sees the glory of people. On some unforgettable evening one's friend is suddenly seen as the unique, irreplaceable, and utterly delightful being that he is. It is as if he had been freshly created. One is no longer concerned with his relations to oneself, with his *pragmatic* value. He exists wholly in his own right; his significance is eternal, and the essential mystery of his being is as fathomless as that of God Himself.

J. W. N. Sullivan (1886–1937), *But for the Grace of God*

10 Regarded by Love

During the two years just before and after I was twenty I had two experiences which led to religious conversion. The first occurred when I was waiting at a bus stop on a wet afternoon. It was opposite the Odeon cinema, outside the station, and I was surrounded by people, shops, cars. A friend was with me. All of a sudden, for no apparent reason, everything looked different. Everything I could see shone, vibrated, throbbed with joy and with meaning. I knew that it had done this all along, and would go on doing it, but that usually I couldn't see it. It was all over in a minute or two. I climbed on to the bus, saying nothing to my friend – it seemed impossible to explain – and sat stunned with astonishment and happiness.

The second experience occurred some months later. I left my office at lunch-time, stopped at a small Greek café in Fleet Street to buy some rolls and fruit, and walked up Chancery Lane. It was an August day, quite warm but cloudy, with the sun glaringly, painfully bright, behind the clouds. I had a strong sense that something was about to happen. I sat on a seat in the garden of Lincoln's Inn waiting for whatever it was to occur. The sun behind the clouds grew brighter and brighter, the clouds assumed a shape which fascinated me, and between one moment and the next, although no word had been uttered, I felt myself spoken to. I was aware of being regarded by love, of being wholly accepted, accused, forgiven, all at once. The joy of it was the greatest I had ever known in my life. I felt I had been born for this moment and had marked time till it occurred.

Monica Furlong (b. 1930), *Travelling In*

————11 Giddy with Happiness————

The weather had changed, it was like early spring, and even warm, as she walked the two miles up from the road in the late afternoon. There were aconites and celandines just pushing up through their green sheaths on the banks. Too early, Ben would say, the snow might come again yet, even in March or April. The woods and coppices were still leafless, branches open-meshed, or else pointing up, thin and dark against the blue-white sky; she could see all the way down between the wide-spaced beech trunks, to the fields below.

But there was something in the air, something, a new smell, the beginning of growth, and, as she walked, she had felt a great happiness spurt up within her, and the countryside had looked beautiful, every detail, every leaf-vein and grass-blade was clear and sharp, it was as though she had been re-born into some new world. There was a change in the light, so that the dips and hollows of the valley that she could see between the gaps in the hedges, as the track climbed higher, up to the common, had changed their shapes, and the colours changed, too, the bracken was soft moss-green and the soil gold-tinged like tobacco. Yesterday, it had been dark as peat.

She wanted to sing. Because she had all she could ever want, the whole earth belonged to her, and in the end, seeing the cottage ahead, she had had to shake her head to clear it, she was giddy with this happiness.

Susan Hill (b. 1942), *In the Springtime of the Year*

12 *Divine Visitations*

When the Lord visits us in the night, what is the effect upon us? When hearts meet hearts in fellowship of love, communion brings first peace, then rest, and then joy of soul. I am speaking of no emotional excitement rising into fanatical rapture; but I speak of sober fact when I say that the Lord's great heart touches ours, and our heart rises into sympathy with Him.

First, we experience *peace*. All war is over, and a blessed peace is proclaimed; the peace of God keeps our heart and mind by Christ Jesus.

> Peace, perfect peace, in this dark world of sin?
> The blood of Jesus whispers peace within.
>
> Peace, perfect peace, with sorrows surging round?
> On Jesus' bosom nought but calm is found.

At such a time there is a delightful sense of *rest*; we have no ambitions, no desires. A divine serenity and security envelop us. We have no thought of foes, or fears, or afflictions, or doubts. There is a joyful laying aside of our own will. We *are* nothing, and we *will* nothing: Christ is everything, and His will is the pulse of our soul. We are perfectly content either to be ill or to be well, to be rich or to be poor, to be slandered or to be honoured, so that we may but abide in the love of Christ. Jesus fills the horizon of our being.

At such a time a flood of great *joy* will fill our minds. We shall half wish that the morning may never break again, for fear its light should banish the superior light of Christ's presence. We shall wish that we could glide away with our Beloved to the place where He feedeth among the lilies. We long to hear the voices of the white-robed armies, that we may follow their glorious Leader whithersoever He goeth. I am persuaded that there is no great actual distance between earth and heaven: the distance lies in our dull minds. When the Beloved visits us in the night He makes our chambers to be the vestibule of His palace-halls. Earth rises to heaven when heaven comes down to earth.

C. H. Spurgeon (1834–1892), *Till He Come*

13   Life

As late I journeyed o'er the extensive plain
  Where native Otter sports his scanty stream,
Musing in torpid woe a Sister's pain,
  The glorious prospect woke me from the dream.

At every step it widened to my sight –
  Wood, Meadow, verdant Hill, and dreary Steep,
Following in quick succession of delight, –
  Till all – at once – did my eye ravished sweep!

May this (I cried) my course through Life portray!
New scenes of Wisdom may each step display,
  And Knowledge open as my days advance!
Till what time Death shall pour the undarkened ray,
  My eye shall dart thro' infinite expanse,
And thought suspended lie in Rapture's blissful trance.

S. T. Coleridge (1772–1834)

14   A Flower Has Opened

A flower has opened in my heart . . .
What flower is this, what flower of spring,
What simple, secret thing?
It is the peace that shines apart,
The peace of daybreak skies that bring
Clear song and wild swift wing.
Heart's miracle of inward light,
What powers unknown have sown your seed
And your perfection freed? . . .
O flower within me wondrous white,
I know you only as my need
And my unsealed sight.

Siegried Sassoon (1886–1967)

15   The Whole World Awake

He said the pleasantest manner of spending a . . . day was
lying from morning till evening on a bank of heath in the middle
of the moors, with the bees humming dreamily about among
the bloom, and the larks singing high up over head, and the
blue sky and bright sun shining steadily and cloudlessly. That
was his most perfect idea of heaven's happiness: mine was
rocking in a rustling green tree, with a west wind blowing, and
bright white clouds flitting rapidly above; and not only larks,
but throstles, and blackbirds, and linnets, and cuckoos pouring
out music on every side, and the moors seen at a distance,
broken into cool dusky dells; but close by great swells of long
grass undulating in waves to the breeze; and woods and sounding water, and the whole world awake and wild with joy.

Emily Brontë (1818–1848), *Wuthering Heights*

16 *Sweet Funeral Bells*

Sweet funeral bells from some incalculable distance, wailing over the dead that die before the dawn, awakened me as I slept in a boat moored to some familiar shore . . .

I sat, and wept in secret the tears that men have ever given to the memory of those that died before the dawn, and by the treachery of earth, our mother. But suddenly the tears and funeral bells were hushed by a shout as of many nations, and by a roar as from some great king's artillery, advancing rapidly along the valleys, and heard afar by echoes from the mountains. 'Hush!' I said, as I bent my ear earthwards to listen – 'hush! – this either is the very anarchy of strife, or else' – and then I listened more profoundly, and whispered as I raised my head – 'or else, oh heavens! it is *victory* that is final, victory that swallows up all strife.'

Thomas De Quincey (1785–1859), 'The English Mail Coach'

17 *One Cold Morning*

On one of the coldest mornings of that spring, after she had learnt from a London specialist that she might not have more than two years to live, she went for a walk past Clare Leighton's cottage to a farm further up the hill. She felt tired and dejected; her mind, still vigorously alive in her slow, impaired body, rebelled bitterly against her fate. Why, she wondered, should she, at thirty-three, not yet in the fullness of her developing powers, be singled out for this cruel unforeseen blow? She knew, for the constant demands of her friends had made it clear to her, that her life was infinitely valuable to others. She thought of all the half-dead people who 'put in time', as though time were not the greatest gift in the universe, while she, who could use it so superbly, was soon to be deprived of it for ever; and she felt that her mind could hardly contain the rising anguish of that realization.

Just then she found herself standing by a trough outside the farmyard; the water in it was frozen and a number of young lambs were struggling beside it vainly trying to drink. She broke the ice for them with her stick, and as she did so she heard a voice within her saying: 'Having nothing, yet possessing all things.' It was so distinct that she looked round, startled, but she was alone with the lambs on the top of the hill. Suddenly, in a flash, the grief, the bitterness, the sense of frustration disappeared; all desire to possess power and glory for herself vanished away, and never came back. She walked down the hill with the exhilaration which, says Storm Jameson in *Civil Journey*, 'springs from the sense of having lost everything. It is a feeling like no other, a curious form of spiritual intoxication, perhaps not repeatable.'

Winifred never told me of this incident nor of the sentence of death passed upon her, until June 1935, when she had only three months to live. By that time she thought – or, as I now suspect, allowed me to believe that she thought – that she had outwitted the doctors. The moment of 'conversion' on the hill at Monks Risborough, she said with tears in her eyes, was the supreme spiritual experience of her life. She always associated it afterwards with the words of Bernard Bosanquet on Salvation:

'And now we are saved absolutely, we need not say from what, we are at home in the universe, and, in principle and in the main, feeble and timid creatures as we are, there is nothing anywhere within the world or without it that can make us afraid.'

Vera Brittain (1893–1970), *Testament of Friendship*

——————— *18   Returning from Church* ———————

O little lark, you need not fly
To seek your Master in the sky,
    He treads our native sod;
Why should you sing aloft, apart?
Sing to the heaven of my heart;
    In me, in me, in me is God!

O strangers passing in your car,
You pity me who come so far
   On dusty feet, ill shod;
You cannot guess, you cannot know
Upon what wings of joy I go
   Who travel home with God.

From far-off lands they bring your fare,
Earth's choicest morsels are your share,
   And prize of gun and rod;
At richer boards I take my seat,
Have dainties angels may not eat:
   In me, in me, in me is God!

O little lark, sing loud and long
To Him who gave you flight and song,
   And me a heart aflame.
He loveth them of low degree,
And He hath magnified me,
   And holy, holy, holy is His Name!

Anna Bunston de Bary (1869–1954)

——— *19 The Sweetness of His Heart* ———

If you think inwardly of the good things God has done for you
and will do for you, and if you would love him entirely, then
you will be stirred to love him more heartily. For when you
were nothing, he made you out of nothing; when you were
lost, he found you; when you were perished, he sought you;
when you were sold to sin he bought you; and when you were
lost eternally, he saved you. When you were born in sin, he
baptised you, and often afterwards when you sinned he bore
with you generously and awaited your amendment, receiving
you sweetly, and through his grace placing you in his sweet
fellowship. Each day when you fall, he reproves you; and when
you repent, he forgives you. When you err, he amends you;
when you doubt, he teaches you; when you hunger, he feeds
you; when you are cold, he warms you; when you are hot, he
cools you; when you sleep, he saves you; and when you get

up, he beholds you; and always when you are ill at ease, he comforts you.

These good things and many more has our Lord Jesus Christ done for you. Consider the sweetness of his heart, and evermore speak of it; and, if you know anything of love, thank him both day and night.

Edmund of Abingdon (c. 1175–1240), *The Mirror of St Edmund*

20 The Bold Strength of Love

In the early days of the Church, in the times of persecution, many people were so wonderfully and unexpectedly touched by grace that, without any previous spiritual experience, craftsmen threw down their tools and children their slates, and ran to be martyred with the saints. That being so, why should not we who live in peaceful times believe that God may, can, will and, indeed, does touch different people just as suddenly with the grace of contemplation? And this I believe he willingly does to chosen souls by the bounty of his grace. For ultimately he will be known for what he is, to the wonderment of the whole world. Such a soul, lovingly reducing itself to nothing and making God everything, is protected from all physical and spiritual foes by the fulness and goodness of God's grace, and not by any effort of its own. For common sense demands that God should keep safe all who for love of him forsake themselves and become indifferent to their own welfare. It is little wonder then that they are so marvellously kept, for they are truly humble in the bold strength of their love.

Anonymous (c. 1370), *The Epistle of Privy Counsel*

Hymn: My Song is Love Unknown

My song is love unknown,
  My Saviour's love to me,
Love to the loveless shown,
  That they might lovely be.

O who am I,
That for my sake
My Lord should take
Frail flesh, and die?

He came from his blest throne,
Salvation to bestow;
But men made strange, and none
The longed-for Christ would know.
But O, my friend,
My friend indeed,
Who at my need
His life did spend!

Sometimes they strew his way,
And his sweet praises sing;
Resounding all the day
Hosannas to their King.
Then 'Crucify!'
Is all their breath,
And for his death
They thirst and cry.

Why, what hath my Lord done?
What makes this rage and spite?
He made the lame to run,
He gave the blind their sight.
Sweet injuries!
Yet they at these
Themselves displease,
And 'gainst him rise.

They rise, and needs will have
My dear Lord made away;
A murderer they save,
The Prince of Life they slay.
Yet cheerful he
To suffering goes,
That he his foes
From thence might free.

In life, no house, no home
  My Lord on earth might have;
In death, no friendly tomb
  But what a stranger gave.
    What may I say?
      Heaven was his home;
      But mine the tomb
    Wherein he lay.

Here might I stay and sing.
  No story so divine;
Never was love, dear King,
  Never was grief like thine!
    This is my friend,
      In whose sweet praise
      I all my days
    Could gladly spend.

Samuel Crossman (1624–1684)

Keep me, O Lord, while I tarry on this earth, in a daily serious seeking after thee and in a believing affectionate walking with thee; that when thou comest, I may be found not hiding my talent, nor yet asleep with my lamp unfurnished; but waiting and longing for my Lord, my glorious God, for ever and ever.

Richard Baxter (1615–1691)

Acknowledgements

We gratefully acknowledge permission to reprint copyright material in this anthology. We apologize to those copyright-holders whom it has proved impossible to locate.

Aelfric: from 'The Passion of St Edmund, King and Martyr' from *Lives of the Saints* in *Anglo-Saxon Prose*, translated and edited by Michael Swanton, J. M. Dent, 1975. Reprinted by permission of the publisher.

Aelred of Rievaulx: from *A Rule of Life for a Recluse* translated by Mary Paul Macpherson ocso in *Treatises and The Pastoral Prayer*, Cistercian Fathers Series no. 2, 1971. Reprinted by permission of Cistercian Publications Inc. WMU Station, Kalamazoo, Michigan 49008.

Anonymous: from 'The Dream of the Rood' translated by Helen Gardner in *The Faber Book of Religious Verse*, 1972. Reprinted by permission of Katherine Duncan-Jones.

Anonymous: from 'Thirty-one Riddles' in *The Anglo-Saxon World*, edited and translated by Kevin Crossley-Holland, Oxford University Press, 1984. Reprinted by permission of Rogers, Coleridge & White Ltd.

George Appleton: from *Journey for a Soul*, Fount Paperbacks, 1977. Reprinted by permission of Collins Publishers.

Catherine Bramwell-Booth: from *Letters*, introduced by Mary Batchelor, Lion Publishing, 1986. Reprinted by permission of the publisher.

Vera Brittain: from *Testament of Friendship: The Story of Winifred Holtby*, Virago Ltd, 1980. Reprinted by permission of Vera Brittain's literary executors.

Anna Bunston de Bary: from *Collected Poems*, The Mitre Press, 1947. Reprinted by permission of Charles Skilton Ltd.

Agatha Christie: from *An Autobiography*, William Collins Sons & Co., 1958. Reprinted by permission of Aitken & Stone Ltd and Harold Ober Associates Inc.

Austin Farrer: from *Lord I Believe*. The Faith Press Ltd, 1958. Reprinted by permission of Cowley Publications.

Monica Furlong: from *Travelling In*, Hodder & Stoughton Ltd, 1971. Reprinted by permission of Monica Furlong and Anthony Sheil Associates Ltd.

Gilbert of Hoyland: from 'Treatise 3: How Joy Differs on the Way and in the Fatherland!' in *The Works of Gilbert of Hoyland* vol. IV translated by Lawrence C. Braceland sj. Cistercian Fathers Series no. 34, 1981. Reprinted by permission of Cistercian Publications Inc., WMU Station, Kalamazoo, Michigan 49008.

Caroline Glyn: from 'Easter at Rendon Castle' in *A Mountain at the End of Night*, Victor Gollancz Ltd, 1977. Reprinted by permission of the publisher.

George H. Gorman: from *Introducing Quakers*, Quaker Home Service, 1974. Reprinted by permission of the publisher.

Susan Hill: from *In the Springtime of the Year*, Hamish Hamilton Ltd, 1974. Reprinted by permission of the publisher and Georges Borchardt Inc.

Michael Hollings: from *I Will be There*, Mowbray, 1975. Reprinted by permission of Cassell plc.

Gerard Manley Hopkins: from *Gerard Manley Hopkins: Poetry and Prose* edited by W. H. Gardner, Penguin 1953. Reprinted by permission of OUP.

Laurence Housman: from *The Unexpected Years*, Jonathan Cape Ltd, 1937. Reprinted by permission of the publisher.

Margery Kempe: from *The Book of Margery Kempe: A Modern Version* by W. Butler-Bowden, OUP, 1954. Reprinted by permission of the publisher.

Francis Kilvert: from *Kilvert's Diary* edited by William Plomer, Jonathan Cape Ltd, 1944. Reprinted by permission of the publisher and Mrs Sheila Hooper.

D. H. Lawrence: from *The Complete Poems of D. H. Lawrence*, edited by Vivian de Sola Pinto and Warren Roberts, William Heineman Ltd, 1964. Reprinted by permission of Laurence Pollinger Ltd and the Estate of the late Mrs Frieda Lawrence Ravagli.

C. S. Lewis: from *The Magician's Nephew*, Fontana Lions, 1980. Reprinted by permission of William Collins Sons & Co. Ltd.

Rose Macaulay: from *Letters to a Friend* edited by Constance Babington-Smith, Collins, 1961. Reprinted by permission of Peters, Fraser and Dunlop.

Wilfred Owen: from *The Collected Poems of Wilfred Owen* edited by Edmund Blunden, Chatto & Windus, 1963. Reprinted by permission of the Executors of Harold Owen's Estate, The Hogarth Press and New Directions Publishing Corporation.

J. B. Phillips: from *The Wounded Healer* edited by Vera Phillip and Edwin Robertson, Triangle/SPCK, 1984. Reprinted by permission of SPCK and Wm. B. Eerdmans Publishing Co.

Bertrand Russell: from 'A Free Man's Worship' in *Mysticism and Logic*, Allen & Unwin, 1976. Reprinted by permission of Unwin Hyman Ltd.

Margaret Sackville: from *Collected Poems*, The Richards Press Ltd, 1939.

Siegfried Sassoon: from *Collected Poems*, Faber & Faber Ltd, 1947. Reprinted by permission of George T. Sassoon.

Dorothy L. Sayers: from *Unpopular Opinions*, Victor Gollancz Ltd, 1946. Reprinted by permission of David Higham Associates Ltd.

Stevie Smith: from *The Collected Poems of Stevie Smith*, Penguin Modern Classics, 1985. Reprinted by permission of James MacGibbon (UK) and New Directions Publishing Corporation (USA).

J. W. N. Sullivan: from *But for the Grace of God*, Jonathan Cape Ltd, 1932. Reprinted by permission of the publisher.

John V. Taylor: from *The Go-Between God*, SCM Press Ltd, 1972. Reprinted by permission of SCM Press (UK) and Oxford University Press, New York.

William Temple: from *Personal Religion and the Life of Fellowship*, Longmans, Green & Co. Ltd, 1926. Reprinted by permission of Longman Group UK Ltd.

Evelyn Underhill: from *Abba*, Longmans, Green & Co Ltd, 1940. Reprinted by permission of Longman Group UK Ltd.

H. G. Wells: from *The Outline of History*, 1923. Reprinted by permission of A. P. Watt Ltd on behalf of the Executors of the Estate of G. P. Wells.

H. A. Williams: from *Becoming What I Am*, Darton, Longman & Todd, 1977. Published in USA by Augsburg Press as *The Simplicity of Prayer*. Reprinted by permission of the publishers.

Wulfstan: from 'The Institutes of Polity' in *Anglo-Saxon Prose* translated and edited by Michael Swanton, J. M. Dent, 1975. Reprinted by permission of the publisher.

The quotations from the Bible near the beginning of each of the six chapters are taken from the Authorized Version.

In addition we wish to thank Margaret Smith, Ann Tilley and Geoffrey and Carolyn Whitney-Brown for their valuable suggestions in compiling this anthology.

Index

Layamon 79–80
Lewis, C. S. 103–4
Lupset, Thomas 57

Macaulay, Rose 97–8
Mansfield, Katherine 57–8
Maurice, F. D. 9
Meyer, F. B. 47
Meynell, Alice 99
Milman, H. H. 22
Milner-White, Eric 109
Milton, John 114
More, Hannah 94–5
More, Thomas 27–8

Newman, John Henry 78–9
Newton, John 53

Overton, Richard 36
Owen, Wilfred 18–19

Phillips, J. B. 50–1

Raleigh, Walter 14–15
Richard of Chichester 87
Robertson, F. W. 54–5
Rolle, Richard 113–14
Rossetti, Christina 72–3
Rowe, Elizabeth 76–7
Royal Maundy, The 23
Russell, Bertrand 58–9

Sackville, Margaret 32
Sassoon, Siegfried 122

Sayers, Dorothy L. 7–8
Smart, Christopher 83
Smith, Stevie 40
Smith, Sydney 13
Spenser, Edmund 91
Spurgeon, C. H. 120–1
Stephen, Caroline 15–16
Stevenson, Robert Louis 16–17
Studdert-Kennedy, G. A. 71
Sullivan, J. W. N. 118

Taylor, Jeremy 35
Taylor, John V. 117
Temple, Frederick 65
Temple, William 30–1
Tennyson, Alfred 116–17
Thackeray, William 81
Thompson, Francis 61
Toplady, A. M. 63
Traherne, Thomas 33

Underhill, Evelyn 31–2

Vaughan, Charles 86
Vaughan, Henry 5
Von Hügel, Friedrich 96

Watts, Isaac 85
Wells, H. G. 9–10
Wesley, Charles 107–8
Westminster School 22
Whitefield, George 78
Williams, H. A. 12
Wulfstan 11–12